An Angler's Album

FROM WATER
TO NET

An Angler's Album
FROM WATER TO NET
John Bailey

DAVID & CHARLES
Newton Abbot   London

British Library Cataloguing in Publication Data
Bailey, John
From water to net: an angler's album
1. Freshwater angling.
I. Title
799.11

ISBN 0–7153–9468–1

Typeset by Ace Filmsetting Ltd, Frome
and printed in Italy by New Interlitho SpA
for David & Charles plc
Brunel House, Newton Abbot, Devon

Contents

Introduction

Around the turn of the 1970s, I was fortunate enough to be living in Norfolk and to be fishing that most beautiful of rivers, the Wensum, when it was producing huge roach in unprecedented numbers. By 1973 I was writing about my exploits, needing photographs and dragging poor old John Wilson, unprotesting it must be said, out with his camera over and over again. Finally, after dozens of errands, he rightly insisted that I bought my own camera. It was essential, he said, if I were to continue writing angling articles. I went up the alley from his tackle den into the nearest shop, and came out with a Russian SLR camera of antique design and great weight. It did, however, have a delayed release facility and so, using my smart new tripod, I could take the shots of myself and the fish I so obviously needed.

I left the City, drove up the valley road, and at last light, I caught a roach. It was a big one of 2lb 7oz. I was overjoyed and set up the camera. I pushed a landing net into the bank for me to focus by and took the required light readings. All was ready. I got the fish from the net and set the camera in motion. Some days later, I got the results back from the photographers:

Frame 1: A landing net standing proud against a gloomy sky. No angler in sight.
Frame 2: The blurred, Barboured backside of an angler pressed against a lens.
Frame 3: A shot of the top of an angler's head as he looks for a roach dropped somewhere in the sedge.
Frame 4: Over-exposed.
Frame 5: Under-exposed.
Frame 6: A worried angler peers at the camera obviously wondering if the shutter is somehow jammed.
Frame 7: A proud angler holds what is probably a roach but which is unfortunately totally out of screen, exiting somewhere stage right.
Frame 8: Angler and fish blurred beyond any possible recognition.

I realised that I needed to improve.

Ever since those early days, photography has become an ever more important part of my angling experience. My cameras and accessories have been constantly updated. That first flashgun was the most essential addition, simply for the good of the fish. From 1975 it has no longer been necessary to keep fish in a net overnight, and the resulting damage to scales and fins has been thankfully avoided. My earlier photos were simply trophy shots taken to satisfy the need for proof-of-the-pudding material that I was told was required. ('Proof-of-the-pudding'—always one of the most stupid phrases in angling journalism!) After a while I realised it was mindbendingly difficult to give variety to simple fish shots like these—especially up to 1976 or so when I was still predominantly roach fishing. Roach held, roach weighed, roach returned, roach at dusk, roach at dawn, roach at night—a roach is a roach is a roach . . . I had to become a little bolder though at first my attempts were feeble and editors mistrusted anything unusual.

Much more important was the fact that my halting camera skills were at least teaching me to appreciate the water world almost constantly around me. Inevitably, ever since childhood, I had been aware of natural beauty, but by the late 1970s I was drinking it in through the camera lens—though constantly unable to capture effectively the wonders that I witnessed.

Of course, all an angler's senses are involved in this life of his: the heavy, rich smell of loosestrife in the dewy dawn; the tang of wild mint crushed by the stool on the overgrown riverbank; the sound of owls calling from the wooded carp lake as night creeps in, and the hedgehog shuffling and snuffling under the rhododendron bush loud as the bogeyman; the taste of soup on a freezing February day by the pike lake; the sandwich at dawn; the beer after a long hot day on the tench lake; and the comfort of a warm, snug bed after a week under canvas on a hard bank. All these things are central, but not perhaps as vivid as the sights flashing constantly around us anglers. An angler knows that water itself is the most amazing of the elements: the tranquil, oil-smeared face of a canal, the eddying peace of the lowland river, the serenity of a mere, and the crashing violence of a loch in a spring gale. Water is ever-changing, reflecting storms, summer skies, hills, castles, dreaming trees or the factories and houses of the cities. White rapids and twisting currents where the water is a visible, strong smooth muscle. Water freckled by a drizzle, or pock-marked and leaden by a downpour. Water chocolate after winter rains. Water so clear it is only apparent as an element at all because the wind ruffles it, a coot splashes it in defiance and because a fish dimples it with a kissing rise.

It is in the eyes of anglers that floats the pure white dagger of grebe; it is they who see the heron of the pond, the eagle of a mountain torrent, the water vole hiding in the old mill race, the otter passing through the swim at dawn, the swans gliding out of the mists of sunrise. And only anglers can see the fish themselves, creatures that ordinary mortals can never even guess at. Fish are as majestic as anything in nature, and even naturalists are so often ignorant of them. The texture of a tench flank, the unique gold of a rudd, the bars of a perch, the cream white of a big pike's belly—beneath the water exists a beauty just as great as the world above it can show. The surface of the water is the frontier. The rod and the line are man's way of crossing the divide. An angler is casting literally into another world, and if he uses his eyes the wonders are great indeed.

Fish basking in the heat; predators striking at dawn; carp leaping out in the dead of night—if ever angling is banned, I for one will still fish on—but with my camera. A fish on film is all but as fine as a fish on the line.

This, then, is the core of the book. It is a record of what my camera saw over a twelve-month period. It records some of the adventures on the waters that I love the most, studying and sometimes catching the fish that are so vitally exciting, with friends who help to make an angler's life such a satisfying and rich one.

I have included every major coarse fish, with one or two surprises like the predatorial brown trout—the ferox—and even a grass carp. My hope is that the photographs and the text will work together to both inspire and instruct. I have put particularly heavy emphasis on the captions to many of the photographs as I feel that one picture can tell so many tales—some all too easily overlooked.

Glorious summer angling

An eternal evening sun settles over the Wensum flood plains

PART I

Ferox Spring

The ferox is a great predatorial brown trout that lives in the deep, cold-water glacial lochs of Scotland, Ireland and Alpine Europe. Ferox feed on char shoals, on smaller trout, on perch, on anything that the mineral-poor waters offer them to sustain their bulk. Make no mistake—these fish are big. A good one is 7lb in weight, a fish of a lifetime is 10lb, the record is 19lb and a possibility, just, is 25lb. A dream is one of 30lb. With size goes the incredible beauty of a natural, indigenous trout that has had nothing to do with stew ponds or pellets. With size and with desirability also goes rarity. There is *no* greater challenge in British freshwater than the ferox. Fly fishing for the most part is impractical. Ferox are the target of the big predator hunter with live or dead bait, spoon or plug. Trolling is the best method to cover the thousands of acres of these forbidding waters.

Almost always things go wrong. Storms blow up out of blue skies. Engines break down miles from base. Rods go overboard in a swell. Boats even capsize. Lines get tangled and lures get snagged. Even when things go right, success is heartbreakingly rare . . . which is why few anglers since the Victorian and Edwardian period have tackled ferox. In those days when the ferox was more widespread, angling writers declared that on average one ferox equalled two hundred trolled miles! Today . . . ? Still, we do have the advantages of engines and echo sounders, and occasionally the combinations click and the safe door to ferox gold opens wide. It did in the spring of 1989, in the Highlands, for a friend of mine.

Bad weather

I had travelled north in March and left an England that was comparatively mild and settled but, as is so often the case, the weather turned as I crossed the borders into Scotland. I had hoped to travel to my far-flung glen within the single day but as dusk pulled in, the wind plucked at the car and the snow began to fall ever more thickly. I looked for a place to sleep but the road by now was dark, deep in white and deserted. It was nearly midnight before I saw a light and knocked at the door of an isolated farm. As is the way with Scottish folk, I was welcomed in and slept sound as the blizzard blew night through.

My hosts begged me to stay with them next morning but I resisted, having decided to push on the final two hundred miles to my hotel where I knew there would be a warm welcome. That journey took all the daylight hours, and into darkness I was following the snow ploughs. Well after dusk I entered the glen and found the hotel safely; but it was again near midnight before I was installed, tired

A full moon does prove a problem in the sense that it brings down temperatures a great deal, and makes winter fishing at dawn and dusk very cold work indeed. However, there is evidence emerging that both the full and the new moon stimulate fish greatly and a good deal of big fish fall at these periods

A day like this spells good fishing for ferox and all predators—if you can stick the cold! The wind kicks up a good ripple on the water which masks the disturbance of the boat and the cloud cover keeps light values down in deep, dark water

The old writers often stated that the true ferox possessed black spots only. Perhaps that was, or is, true in some waters where the strain has developed in its own special way, or perhaps the black spotted ferox was a myth current amongst the misinformed and largely ignorant. Certainly, of the twenty or thirty ferox I have studied, a good few have at least a few red spots

out, in a garret room of the old shooting lodge. A full moon shone, the skies were alternately clear or snow-laden, and a strong wind blew at the windows. The view looked out over the gleaming river that ran from the ferox loch situated high up in the mountains to the west. The night was bitterly cold and I huddled in the big brass bed with hot water bottle, a hot toddy and, fittingly, a gothic horror novel. But for me, the owner and his family, and the notorious ghost reputed to live in Room 7, the hotel was empty, shivering on the hillside. There was no sound but the weather without and the odd creaking of old beams, and I slept sound until mid-morning.

There was little light the next day when I pulled back the curtains. The glen was draped under grim skies and snow was still piling down. The lane outside was deep and white with no sign of tyre marks upon it. Down in the kitchen by the cooking range, the owner confirmed what I well knew: we were cut off, and everything now would depend upon the weather.

For the following days, I trekked the glen by foot. Blizzards were frequent and when they came the whole world was obliterated in whiteness. The sky would darken towards the west and the wind would rise from a moan to a howl. The gleams of a pale sun would be slowly strangled out and within minutes a veil of white would sweep down the glen. Over and over, I was caught outside and forced to shelter in ruins, bothys or on the lee of any natural shelter. The cold would be frighteningly intense. Once I fell into a sleep so deep that it was nearer a faint or even a coma; I was woken only by the shuffling of deer seeking the same refuge of

14

old walling as I, in hard times overlooking their natural fear of man The animals were suffering desperately from the prolonged winter. Previous months of wetness had worn down their energies and now this further blow was reducing their reserves ever further. Their frames were spare, their coats dulled and their eyes listless; the yearlings especially looked all but done in.

It was impossible to fish the lochs during these days, and all I could do was to try the river later on in the afternoons when the days had warmed up sufficiently for me to contemplate standing in the freezing snow-water. I would stick it out till the night fell and the moon rose splendidly over the mountain range, turning the river to flowing diamonds; but I remained fishless. However, I hardly expected much to move under these frost-gripped conditions.

A week passed, and little by little the wind grew less keen and the temperatures began to rise. Miraculously, one morning, there was full sunlight and a sky blue from peak to peak. That was the day the roads cleared and I began to make ready for trolling at last.

The checklist of a troller's gear is immense: an engine, and perhaps if you are prudent and wealthy enough, a spare; petrol; oars; rowlocks; rodrests; rods and reels; haversacks of gear; maps of the lochs; torches and nets; boots, waterproof suits and life jackets; echo sounders; and something in the way of food and drink—all these take hours to assemble. When alone, just loading the boat with everything is a back-breaking job.

The glacial loch is a frightening place to fish at any time—never mind when the snow lays thickly. Depths can be immense—well over 200 feet—and the sides can shelve to over 100 feet deep just a few boat lengths from the bank

There is no doubt that the first hours of darkness can pay off handsomely. The lowering light values encourage the big trout to move from their daytime lairs, and to search for food actively. Wading, like this, and casting an 18 or 20 gramme Toby into the pools can bring a fish at any moment. Do take care, though —for your safety's sake and for your fishing. A false footstep, a dislodged rock and either you are in the river or the ferox is scared

This is the reality of a ferox loch at the start of the season. The shot was taken at 3000 feet, and the loch is actually a mile wide down there. Safety is essential. The boat and engine must be totally reliable, safety life jackets must be worn, and you must tell people where you are fishing in case of an accident or being marooned

Highland inhabitant

The typical ferox loch is a barren place and the water tends to be acidic. Ordinary trout tend to be on the lean side and ferox only exist because of the very large char shoals that patrol the lochs. These fish average 4 to 8 ounces and, by their very number, make for reasonably easy hunting

It was fortunate that by then I had John Hett—a fellow ferox freak—along with me. The sun beat down on us as we sped up the loch towards our favourite early season fishing grounds. There we had some luck with smaller trout, with fish to 2 or even 3lb that fell to the lures—but fell also well short of the targets we had set ourselves. The fish that showed up on the echo sounder screen were down deep and we had to troll with spoons heavily leaded. Rappalas, Tobys and big Vincent-type spoons all got takes, but many of the fish came short or were hardly pricked and merely bounced the rod over.

For some reason the mouths of the feeder streams seemed profitable, which was strange considering the ice water that they were disgorging into the loch. There in the small valleys, the full toll of the blizzards could clearly be seen in the carcasses freshly uncovered by the thaw. Dotted along the shore-line deer lay peacefully, alone or in groups, in the very position where they had fallen and entered into eternal sleep. Often their eyes had been eaten out by the hooded crows, but their ears were still pricked as though listening to the stream and winds of the corries.

Those nights spinning the river were exceptional. The big moon seemed to dance off the snow-clad peaks and throw whole handfuls of stardust onto the water. The deeper rapids are also worth investigating. Many small fish hang there, and the big predators are naturally attracted

Notice the map of the area, invaluable for any troller. It can help him in a mist or by showing the quickest routes around these vast waters. A cushion is also useful for a man spending 12 to 14 hours in a boat

John Hett, a frequent boat partner of mine, shows how to arrange the tackle. Everything is laid out for immediate access— essential in a crisis or heavy waves

These feeder streams can also be good holding areas later in the year, around September, for many of the ferox use them as spawning beds and they are beginning to congregate there then

The weather eases

The sun grew hotter, the days lengthened visibly and the daffodils began to nod in the breezes. It was during this lovely time that Norrie arrived, bringing with him the two Johns from Edinburgh. To describe the hugeness of Norrie's size, generosity, warmth and appetite for strong liquor in words is all but impossible. He is, though, a giant of a Scot, soft-spoken and loyal, fun to be with those long days afloat or even longer nights in the bar. The two Johns were of the same sort, dedicated to the Highlands and to fish. They, too, badly wanted ferox and we talked long about them that first night. Considering how deep the echo sounder had shown the big trout to be lying, they decided, sensibly, to troll a dead trout very slowly, heavily leaded and at great depth. The setup that they used was a comparatively simple one, consisting merely of a wire trace (ferox have teeth like pike) and three trebles attached around a central swivel. The top hook goes in the lips of the bait, the second around the area of the gills, and the third is embedded in the flank down towards the tail. The theory is that wherever the ferox takes hold, a hook will penetrate.

Ferox success

For some days, the lads and I trolled tirelessly in weather that was generally calm, often fine but always with the menace of storms and lingering snow. We were all catching fish, small ones true, but enough to keep us going out when the days looked especially dire. The great morning, however, blew in gusty but bright,

A glorious spring day

A small dead trout like this can be loaded with 1 to 3 ounces of weight to make it troll at great depths, where it will still twist and flash even when moved slowly. Two hooks are around the head of the bait as this is where most ferox make their attack

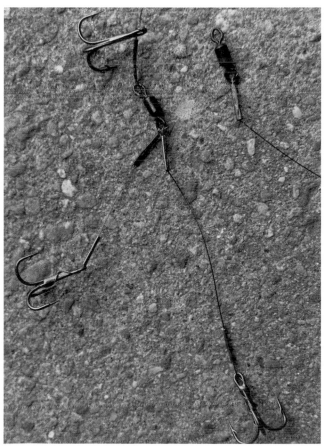

A trace takes a good deal of strain, and the wire should be around 20lb breaking strain. The swivel too should be stout—around 30–50lb test. We prefer the use of barbed hooks, though others believe that barbless points penetrate the bone-jawed ferox more easily

It is rare for me to kill trout but sometimes the hotel is glad of a few for the table. The fish finder is my constant friend, forever telling me the nature of the loch beneath. They are hardy, reliable and simple to use, and no troller should be without one

Three in a small boat is not always a safe proposition, but here the day was calm for once. Also the three are all experienced and keep to their central positions so that the boat is perfectly balanced

Even on cold days like this, sun glasses can combat surface glare and help you look into the sun

A very fine day can also be productive. It could be that the sunlight floods the water and hampers the usual keen sight of the ferox. Certainly, in such conditions the use of a very dark coloured lure is recommended

This is a dangerous moment. The ferox feels the gravel underneath him and he is likely first to kick and then explode away again. It is exactly the time when a failing hook hold will finally give

A close-up of the ferox mouth reveals jaws that carry a multitude of small, needle-sharp teeth. They act like a file on nylon line and necessitate the use of wire traces

At the time, I looked only for black spots and believed that is what I saw. Over a year on, I wonder now, are there flecks of red around the anal fin? The huge spread of the perfectly formed tail explains the massive power of these fish

dazzling clear with sun bouncing off the snow-clad peaks. I had decided to try a lower loch and was fishing there in mid-morning when I heard the horn of a car half a mile above me on the track. It was the ferox trollers, waving and calling me in.

Glad I was that they found me, for there along the back seat of their car lay a ferox, between eight and nine pounds and perfect in every spot and fin. On the way back home, John the captor told me every detail of the catch. The first troll of the morning and the fish had taken, just nudging at the rod tip a couple of times and then holding it down resolutely. John had struck at once at this, but had hooked, he felt, into the bottom. This is a typical initial response to the hooked ferox, as it hangs deep and dour, resisting the boat with bewilderment and following it at last only slowly and grudgingly: then the fish will explode! In John's case, his rod was down to the water and his reel was screaming as his fish plummeted through the clear icy depths; the excitement in the boat was immense as what was obviously a big one took more and more line off the reel. The trout was on the bottom, bumping the leads against rocks, rubbing the line against the old stumps of a drowned forest. Then he was up and running, and the boat was pushing through the waves after him.

Not for twenty minutes did the fish begin to show, glinting in the April sunshine as he turned and struggled to dive a life-saving last time. Norrie manoeuvred the boat to the shore and John played out the final moments in shallow water where they could see the ferox run still. Then it was all over. The fabulous fish lay in the sunlight, for once—forever—out of his element.

News spread up and down the glen. Everybody flocked to see the prize and the drinks flowed early that day. Ferox lay on a silver platter and he was weighed and measured a dozen times. His proportions were perfect—neither fat nor thin, but a bullet-shaped sleekness, designed for a life following the char shoals of the big loch. His spots, as the old writers had foretold, were ferox-black only and showed none of the red of lesser fish. The adipose fin was especially massive—not a stump, a weedy and forgotten reminder of a distant requirement, but a powerful tool in the hunter's life.

Celebrations went on until the small hours of the next day. Songs resounded, tales were told, and the fish was a thousand times toasted. It was a day not often seen in the glen: a ferox, after all, had fallen!

Many of us put ferox back alive, for it seems a tragedy to eat a creature like this. However, this was to be set up for a glass case. Once the fish is dead, lay it flat in a deep freeze, on a board preferably, and wrap it well in cling film to prevent freezer burn. Take care of the fins, which are very brittle and can snap, on the journey to the taxidermist

The enormous adipose fin on a ferox is much bigger than the very small and useless adipose on a lowland trout

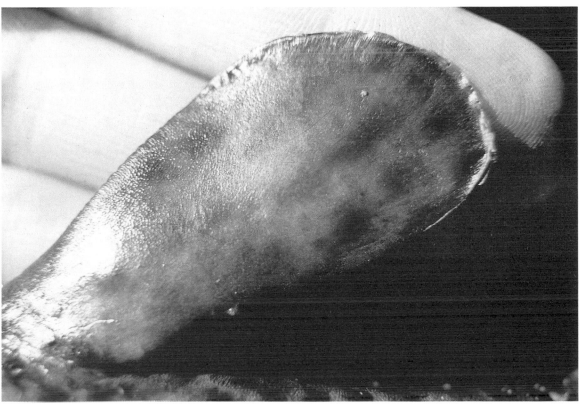

PART II
The Love of a River

Roderick Haig Brown called rivers 'the veins of life'. Most probably he meant this to be taken environmentally but I sometimes wonder if he intended it personally. Perhaps, even, the person and the river can in some way merge; and so this seems for me, and my relationship to the River Wensum in Norfolk.

Early days

All through the August of 1960 it seemed that I stood on the threshold of a dream, on an ancient bridge that spanned my river. These important days of my memory were blissfully fine, spent under a constantly lark-filled blue sky, amidst poppy-freckled corn fields. The sun blazed from its rise to set, sprinkling the crystal river water with gold dust particles and igniting the long gravels to a white blaze.

Fish swarmed there. Schools of minnows finch-flitted in the cover of the reeds. Pike passed through, all mottled, shovel-nosed menace, and packs of brightly barred perch marauded here and there amongst the banners of weeds that rippled on the easy current. Under the trailing fronds of a great white willow a trout rose for moths every happy twilight. There was also a shoal of roach that hung in the shadow of the parapet, and more than all the other fish, these graceful beings captivated me. In the stream of sunlight their scales shone an amber gold and they glowed with life, ever a-twitch on firebird red fins.

Whole weeks passed, my life mesmerised by the heat and the beauty of the water-meadow world. I took breakfast, dinner and supper in a trance by the water-side whilst my legs and arms browned in the sun, my hair bleached yellow-white like wheat. The bridge, the willow, the gentle curve of the beloved river were all my horizons and they remained my very life, long after I was forced to leave them.

An elderly man was my guardian these daylight hours my parents were away. His was the toll cottage beside the bridge, and his labrador smelled of warmth, baked earth and cheese stolen from an unguarded luncheon box. The toll keeper knew then what it took me years to realise for myself, that these roach were far beyond my infant attempts to catch them, that my hook was like an anchor to them and my line like hawser rope. However, I hardly expected to catch fish. To be at one with them, sharing in the shade of the willow was enough. When, later in the month, my float did slither under and the smallest of the roach flashed first in the water and then in the sunlight I had all the success that I ever needed. In such a way did I find the Wensum.

By August 1970 I was a student and wrote to the farm encompassing my river for summer work. Now I was a capable fisherman, and I was quite happy to labour in the potato fields or the cattle sheds through the brightness of the day, knowing that dusk would see the roach feed in earnest. Even after leaving my work, I was in

Bridge swims very often hold good fish. The current tends to speed up and scour out attractive, deep pools

A perfectly formed and coloured roach

Twenty years ago, a centre pin reel was the natural tool for river fishing, and a good deal of pride was attached to using one properly. It did take practice—and a line guard was very useful—but once the centre pin was mastered, it gave superb line control in running water

An upper river in summer can possess a daunting amount of weed, but this does make for healthy food and therefore fish stocks. A careful approach to the water is vital as it is always gin clear and you need to get close to the fish to present a weed-free bait

no hurry to fish, content to talk to the aged toll keeper by his porch, looking down the river where the silvery dace rose with the hatching fly and the trout still plopped under the willow. When the sun was right down, when shadows all melted into a greater dusk, and the sweet smell of high summer was brought to exquisite height by the night's seeping dampness, I knew it was time to begin. Now that I better understood the river, I could merge, invisible with its reeds and rushes, still, silent on the shred of sacking until midnight or beyond. I chose the same pitch always and weaned those same magnificent roach to a diet of bread so that they forgot their snails and caddis. Nightly now, they drifted to my feet where they knew the creamy white flakes would await them. As a child I had had my nose pressed against the window of the riverside, but now I was unlocking all its doors. Scraps of my bread in the reeds attracted the voles, and the voles drew in the owls and a lone badger. My bread in the water attracted the roach, and the roach drew in the otters—on three successive nights I heard them whistle in the darkness, and saw their bodies cut black across the moonlight gleam. Once I had reached out to the river and now it was responding, embracing me as one of its own. I caught roach, several of them, all wonderful fish, held a moment under the starlight and then lovingly returned: for me, then, the dream had become reality.

A passion for roach

Now I was coming to terms with the River Wensum, and the next step obviously was to live on its banks. I settled on a little white cottage in a village half-way up the river valley. The obvious advantage was that it was merely a hundred yards from the river—but the equally obvious disadvantage was that it adjoined a fish and chip shop. At times, these disadvantages seemed to outweigh the advantages! The noise on a Friday or a Saturday night after the pubs had closed was sleep-shattering. More annoyingly still, my van parked cosily under my window was stolen—or borrowed—a couple of times to take some farm labourer to his remote hamlet up the valley. Worse, though, was to come. The owners bought an inhuman incendiary device—a neon light—an insect-attracting glare that hummed all night through but for the hisses given out when a moth fried itself in a scorched death beneath my room.

The advantages of the cottage, however, were immense—they had to be! Firstly there was my house partner, J.J.; he seemed to share all my passions, for the river, the big roach, and the countryside around, and the house always had an air of expectancy about it. J.J. worked shifts and we only ever met up when work and roaching and sleep allowed it. Our friendship was often conducted then by notes, his left on my chair and mine on his. 'Blanked again.' Or, 'A two-pounder first cast at the old mill.' Or, 'One bite missed on the big bend.' And so we kept in touch for a year, apart from our weekly, riotous Saturday nights. John Wilson was often a guest there, and we would drink and talk roach sometimes until dawn. God help the women around us then! I don't think we ever got drunk—the sessions were simply too long for that. On several occasions after John had gone, J.J. and I would simply shake ourselves and get down to the river for a dawn session. It was after one of these sprees that I did come home in a hurry—I found a large, pink flamingo in my swim and I feared that at last the drinking had caught up with me. I was sobered for a fortnight, even after we found out the bird was an escapee from a wildlife park down the valley!

J.J. holds one of his big roach. The river behind him is a perfect roach swim. The water level is dropping after a winter's flood, and the visibility will be 10 to 18 inches. On John's bank, there is a deep, slow eddy that all fish species find attractive, especially in the high water. Opposite is a line of alder trees and roach love to hang in underwater roots and branches

These fish fell at dawn—nearly as good a time as dusk—to double maggot on a size 16, float fished in a small eddy. Bites were very timid, typical for cold conditions. Once the sun got up, sport switched off completely, showing again how vital an early start can be

The search for a 3lb roach

Roach, roach and more roach—that was how our life was then. We fished every day for them, wandered the river constantly, and talked of nothing but roach and dreamed of roach. Especially the fabled three pounder. There was something of a race on for that fish: we all came close with big two pounders, and I had a score or more over 2lb 12oz, and a friend, a great roach man Jimmy Sapey, had one of 2lb 15¾oz! We were all quite obsessed, and J.J.'s card to me at Christmas 1976 went 'Here's to a roach of a pound and another pound and another pound!'

Perhaps it was the card that did it, but in early January I moved to a huge, deep bend. We had fished it before again and again and blanked, but once the year before I had seen a very large fish roll there. That New Year I fished the swim thirty-three times before I had a bite; the fish was 2lb 13oz. Thereafter the trickle of big fish grew. There was only one fish under 2lb 10oz, and most were between 2lb 12oz and 2lb 15oz, a weight I twice recorded.

I felt utterly confident that the swim would produce a three pounder for me, and so it did, one warm March evening when the end of the season was drawing perilously close. A little after darkness I took a 2lb 10oz roach and, I fear to say now, cursed it roundly, fearing it would end the night's action for me. An hour

Opposite: A typical winter roach river. The banks are bare of cover, but the big deep bends offer shelter to the fish wanting to avoid the current. Weather conditions are good. There is hazy sunshine to warm the water, but a decent cloud cover to stop quick heat loss at dusk

This superb bag of fish came at the back end of the season. Around February and March, the roach shoals gather together ready for spawning, and big catches of fish can be made. The usual spawning sites are just upriver of mills where the water is wide and deep. Some fish, however, make for quicker water so it pays to check out both types of area

My 3lb 2oz roach
A perfect morning with only a little downriver breeze and generous cloud cover to keep down light levels

A winter sunset and every roach fisher should be out. The flow is evenly paced and the run is about 5 feet deep—perfect roach water

passed. Two hours—it was nearing 10pm when the bobbin sauntered upwards. The fish felt instantly heavy, so much so I feared a stray bream. But it rolled and I saw it clear in the torch beam and near panicked with the netting. It weighed 3lb 4oz on my scales and 3lb 2oz on J.J.'s scales. I settled for that latter weight. I walked up and down the river all the rest of the night waiting for first light and J.J. with the cameras (one of the rare fish I did not trust to flashlight). It was a grey morning, but exactly at sunrise the clouds parted and there was a five-minute burst of light that set the marsh afire. I have never been as happy in my entire life as I was then. The fish went back into the river, and then I went off to teach for the day exhilarated and tireless—even that next night I did not sleep for excitement. I fear we were a little mad in those days.

The facts of the roach's life

We did learn about roach. We caught hundreds and we watched thousands and we discussed deeply everything that we witnessed. We got to know which swims big roach like: deeper areas with some flow, and a bottom of sand or gravel with some shelter in the form of overhanging trees, floating rafts, water cabbages or a sharp-cut underwater shelf. We got to know where the roach tended to be at different times of the year: upstream of the mills at the back end of the season, beneath the mills in the spring, and often half-way between the mills throughout the summer and the autumn. We got to know when roach feed the best: 4–8am and 9pm until midnight June through to August; 6–9am and 7–11pm for the rest of the year. We learned not to worry too much about the conditions, as some roach will feed every day within these periods. We got to know how roach took a piece of flake: invariably it would be held in their lips a second and then engulfed, the fish moving away. The bobbin would jump initially, and then soar away to the butt.

We studied the biology of the roach carefully. We learned that up until 1967 the river had held huge stocks of good average-sized fish; that columnaris disease had then struck, stocks were cut back, but that the survivors had grown on to become huge. Many of our big fish showed the scars of columnaris, by then healed up but still horrific to look at. We learned it took eight to ten years in the Wensum for a roach to become 2 to 2½lb, and that after reaching maximum size around twelve years of age it could live on for a further five, ten or even more years. We learned to spot the difference between roach and hybrids by looking at lips, fin positions, colorations, scale patterns and overall body shape.

In the winter, roach often head to the city reaches of a river. There the water is often a little warmed by factory discharges and there is a great deal of cover provided by moored boats. The fish are also used to anglers' baits, and the free food thrown in by pedestrians

Typical, old columnaris scars. Very many fish were caught like this with patches of scales removed by the disease and in other areas hard, red blisters gathered in clumps. The roach appeared to have recovered and fought well

The river's problems

We also realised that in many sections the river was facing severe problems. Over many miles, the only roach to be caught or to be seen were big ones. Small fish were either few or non-existent, and by 1978, any roach found away from the one or two well known, still 'hot' areas was a prize. In those days we put forward all manner of explanations: the disease had made the roach impotent or barren; the abandonment of eel traps had resulted in more eels eating more roach eggs;' there had been an explosion of jackpike which were eating the fingerlings; agricultural, industrial and human wastes were poisoning the river; a massive surge of pollution had flushed through the river in the spring; when we were not constantly on the banks as we were at other times.

Fishing results got poorer and poorer, and only falteringly did we arrive at the knowledge we have today: that the dredger is the main culprit in the decline of the Wensum and other lowland rivers like it. This cursed machine widens and deepens the river and thereby reduces the summer flows; the push of water is therefore not enough to flush the river bed, and algae builds up there. This is made worse by agricultural run-off and treated sewage which have enriched the river and promoted horrendous algae growth—the true sand gravel or chalk bottom is masked

It certainly pays to wander any river in search of roach shoals. Polaroid glasses are essential. A bucket for bait, a small tackle bag for floats, shots and hooks, a rod and a net are all the tackle required and you can wander for miles. In summer, roach often seek out quicker, oxygenated water around weirs and mills

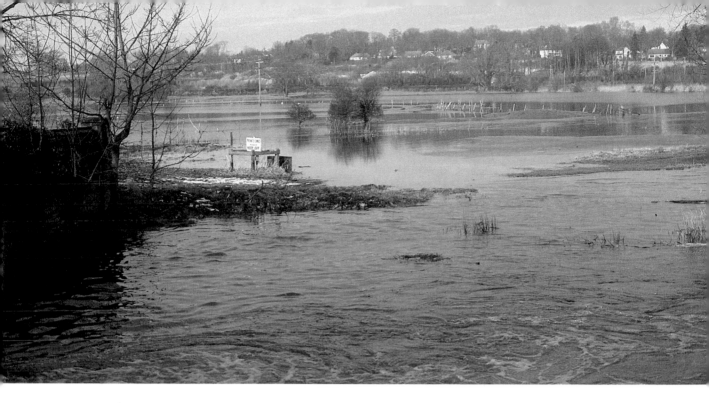

Rising water is rarely worth fishing but as the river drops back into banks and the colour fines down, fish can feed hard on larger, smellier baits like sausage meat and cheese paste

A summer cattle drink is a good barometer of a river's health. If the gravels teem with fry and small fish then the river is healthy. If, however, there are not small fish here then they will not be anywhere, and it is obvious that there are year groups missing in the fish age ladder

This 3lb 10oz monster roach fell, typically, on the point of darkness to a piece of bread flake on a size 10 hook, which was legered on the crease between slack and main river

by algae over many miles, and the roach lose most of their feeding grounds.

In the winter, the rains swell the dredged river massively and it floods—the dredger has swept away all cover, and it roars through the mills, taking with it the defenceless fry of the previous summer. In every way, then, the dredger has destroyed the habitat of the river roach; it has even ripped away the old cattle drinks that warmed up quickly in the summer and gave the roach fry the warm areas they needed within this generally cold chalk spring-fed water system.

If proof of all this is necessary, five minutes only is needed. Stand on the Wensum bridge at Alderford in the middle valley: beneath, the river flows through the estate of a rich industrialist and it has never been dredged. The result is 'bootiful'! There are vast areas of clean gravel, and willows and alders overhang everywhere. There are extensive shallows and deep pools, there is ribbon weed and ranunculus, and algae is hardly present anywhere. Fry team in the margins, roach abound, so do chub, trout and that living barometer of a water's purity, the

44

grayling. There the true Wensum still exists, forbidden, of course, to the true roach man but at least saved for those who care to see it.

Of course, love does not depend on good times alone and even in her decline, I could hardly have considered a divorce from the Wensum. I continued fishing the river for roach, knowing well that very occasional massive fish would be living on here and there, either alone or in tiny groups. In the mid-1980s Roger Miller and I had found one or two promising areas, and were baiting up and fishing on a nightly basis once again. It was almost like the good life of a decade earlier, though more sombre and serious; we were after ultimate prizes we knew, but it was sad stuff, picking around in the ashes of the river corpse. The fishing was diabolically difficult—even my run of thirty-three biteless sessions began to seem easy to us then. For months on end we caught nothing; and then a final burst of three fish—3lb 3oz, 3lb 5oz and 3lb 10oz—proved us to have been absolutely right in our beliefs: there were occasional monsters to be had—and who knows, in those days six years back there could even have been records present in the Wensum . . .

Living with Wensum barbel

The Wensum was never a roach river only. Big, wild brown trout lived in the mill pools, the canniest fish I have ever known, but they could be tempted at night with a crayfish bounced through the pool. There were huge dace, big pike, and of course the nationally famous barbel of the lower river. The Mill House at Costessey was a bittersweet place to live; the river runs right through the gardens, right against the wall of the house, so I was living with it, on it, constantly. Furthermore, the great barbel swim of the river was in the meadow beneath the house, where the river joined up again after running through the mill. Now, at last, I could really get down to the barbel fishing that I wanted so badly in 1979; and that year barbel, to a degree, consoled me for the loss of the roach in the river.

But as I hinted, life at the mill was not always fine. A beauty spot close to a City is a difficult place to live in in a hot summer. Ice-cream vans, swimmers, courting couples, barking dogs, youths on motorbikes and gypsies from a nearby encampment all made heatwaves problematic. We were woken more than once in the early hours by revellers swimming outside our very window, and once at one o'clock in the morning by a man chain-sawing our trees down for wood. I used to keep my rods ready made up in a coalshed for spur-of-the-moment sessions, and had them stolen on three occasions.

The barbel meadow was owned by the family in the big house opposite, a grand mid-Victorian mansion that dominated our humble abode like a castle over a straw hut. They were marvellous to me though, and the key to the meadow gate was in my permanent possession. The barbel lived under a screen of trees whose trailing branches gathered up debris and created a permanent raft. Beneath this, day long, you could see the barbel lined up—big fish, all golden-scaled and tangerine-finned, nosing the current waiting for food to be introduced. Then, when the hemp, the maggots and the sweetcorn were piled in, out they could come, fighting off the chub and digging deep in the sand for the particles. And that is how we caught them—under the rod tip it was easy.

This was only after a first day of horrifying errors: a Sunday in June and I was up at first grey damp light and out on to the meadow. By 5am I had several barbel feeding, and around 6am I hooked one, only for the bend to straighten. Farewell

45

A clean stone bottom attracts insects that in their turn draw in roach, chub and barbel. All these fish like clear beds and will rarely feed over mud and blanket weed

A stunned crayfish, hooked on a size 4 through the tail, is an excellent bait for chub and big trout. They should be used with discretion today, however, as often stocks are low

Barbel search out the quicker, oxygenated runs of a river

In May, the chub gather on the gravel shallows in their hundreds to spawn

to my first-ever barbel! Just before breakfast I was into a second, held it from the snags opposite me—and then the line snapped like pistol shot. I was desolate. I brooded the day out, made up stronger gear and got back in the early wet evening. At 8pm I was into my third barbel, held him hard and the hooks pulled out! At 10pm the fourth and biggest of the day took my bait. I played him to the weed bed at my feet, and there he stuck, head above water, anchored immovably. In I waded to my chest and out I clambered, net full of weed, half a hundredweight of it, but no barbel! That was another night I could not sleep after events on the Wensum.

A barbel catch

There were two sons in the big house, one small and the other tiny, but both showed interest in fishing even then. Ten years on that tiny one, Chris, has made a name for himself with those very fish, from that very swim that *he* has now mastered. He opened the gate to the meadow for me, and the swim was just as I had left it—the barbel might never have moved in all that time, simply remaining there feeding and growing larger. In went the food—again the mix of sweetcorn and hemp but now with wheat added—and out came the barbel legion, flashing on the gravels as they fed beneath the hosts of chub. Eight fish, now ten fish

Opposite: Take the greatest care of a barbel on the bank. A micromesh net is essential. Anything bigger catches and rips the delicate fins. A barbel's mouth is very firm and fleshy, and a disgorger or forceps should always be used for hook extraction

At this stage, you have to keep a hooked barbel moving. If he lodges in weed, the game is probably up

A big barbel is a very fine fish indeed. Its barbules are clearly visible around the mouth. These sensitive feelers can detect insects and baits deep in the sand or gravel

A perfect barbel swim. Barbel are rarely far away from overhead cover and trailing branches form a raft that they find irresistible

Chris feeds heavily with sweetcorn, hemp and wheat to draw the barbel out of the snags onto the clean gravel where a bait can be put to them

After a few minutes, barbel emerge, digging frantically in the stones for food. They still keep close to the trailing weed for cover and can be hard to see

A barbel full on the feed becomes a frantic creature, and often rubs its flank hard along the gravel, perhaps out of excitement, perhaps to stir up food hidden in crevices. Loose feed introduced tightly by a bait dropper seems to produce fierce feeding more quickly than if the bait is scattered by hand

Sequence continues on page 54

appeared, most doubles. Perhaps there were a couple of eight- or nine-pound barbel, but there were some over eleven pounds for sure. They were great gorgeous fish, some pale, one or two dark, and one a deep mahogany brown, all digging furiously for their lunch. There is a pale fish, almost an albino, going frantic, twisting on the bed in ecstasy as it shovels in the grains of wheat.

Chris waits and waits until the fish become crazy for the food, oblivious to us or anything above them. His gear is solid and four tiny pieces of luncheon meat are threaded on to the line above the hook, leaving the point bare. He casts at last—no, not a cast, for the sound of splashing lead will scatter the fish; rather he lowers the bait into the swim beneath the rod tip where the barbel jostle over the food bed. Just the line entering the water makes a barbel back away a foot or so. Chub are a problem, constantly mouthing the bait until Chris shakes it out of their puzzled lips. Eels are even worse, snaking from the weed cover and almost invisible, grabbing the meat in seconds.

At last a barbel comes close, snout over the meat; but he senses a line and he bolts, taking six fish with him. More and more bait goes in and the barbel cannot resist—out they sweep, rooting up the gravel towards the hook bait again. A lovely fish is in the lead. It sees the bait. It pauses. It hovers. It sucks the bait in and hell breaks out. Chris nets it, weighs it, measures it, and carefully returns it to the river. He is shaking. It has got to him, this barbelling! He loves the river like me now he is a man.

River bream

There were always bream in the river, only occasional ones, true, but always big when they came out. They seemed to favour the mill pools of the deepest, darkest, stillest bends where I came to suspect they lived out their entire lives. J.J. had a whacker in 1975, and then in 1979 and 1980 I hit on a shoal of fish a mile downstream of J.J.'s bream. It was in the February, a mild one, that I really hit gold and from that one swim I had four fish between 7lb and 9lb 6oz, held lovingly, I remember, by Dominic, an old pupil. Though the bream did not possess the glamour of roach for me, they were big fish and very greatly appreciated.

Exactly ten years later Roger Miller and I made for the same swim and, hard to believe, the same fish were there still. One fish was the same for sure because that 9lb 6oz bream had a mark below its pectoral fin—the mark quite clearly seen beneath the fin of the 11lb 10oz fish I caught with Roger.

Now, I tell this tale for several reasons: firstly, I find it interesting that bream will remain resident in a river hole all their lives and grow steadily; but even more fascinating are their feeding habits. These bream are ridiculously hard to catch, and even though they roll there in front of you, a bite becomes something of an event at times. Dawn was obviously favoured, and so was the first hour of darkness, but there were no guarantees of action even if you sat there all night, as I did, twice. There were a great number of fry in the slack at the head of the pool, and on milder nights they dimpled the surface constantly. They had obviously attracted pike, for slashing attacks were common in rapid bursts ten minutes or so apart. Well into the winter, something struck me as unusual about the strikes. They seemed too noisy and splashy for pike, I felt, and I began to suspect the possibility of a perch shoal at work. Accordingly, I sat on the bank well away from my rod, my torch beam playing into the clear river. The fry were easily visible, glinting like

Large river bream are dramatic fish. They often fight well and are not as slimy as stillwater fish

Roger Miller is an excellent river fisherman. Here, he is relaxed in a comfortable chair, prepared for a long session. The tip of his rod is painted white for better visibility in the dusk and the night. His tackle is handily laid around him and he has a thick warm suit on for when the temperatures fall

Continued from page 51

Chris keeps low beneath the skyline—vital if the barbel are to feed close in. He legers right under his rod tip so as little line as possible is in the swim. Educated barbel can see and feel it easily

A hooked barbel has to be hustled immediately away from danger otherwise he will be lost in the tree roots. A powerful, through actioned rod, 8 to 10lb line and the strongest hooks are necessary for the job

If possible, get the barbel going upriver. This will tire him faster and if he does get into weed, then he can be pulled out from below

The fish is nearly beaten and it is vital to keep the head up at this stage

Success at last

Chris is very particular over the weighing, measuring and recording of any identifying marks on his barbel. He regards it very much as a scientific exercise to study the individual's growth and movement patterns

All barbel should be held like this until they show the power and inclination to move off into the current and hold their position there. Too many barbel are released back exhausted—only to roll over, be swept downriver and perhaps die as a result

This bream is a monster for a river. Usually, bream from running water do well to reach 5 or 6lb

needles in the top layers of water. I waited a mere five minutes before four shapes glided into the beam, five feet down and rising quickly. They, of course, were big bream and they hit into the fry like bats from hell's dark depths; chasing, harrying them, and sinking back down with at least one fish each in their mouths. Naturally, I tried little live and dead baits a great deal thereafter and it would be nice, but completely untrue, to say that that is how I caught more bream. However, apart from a jackpike and two eels nothing else touched them, so it was back to bread and worms and the occasional big fish pulling the quiver tip round.

Notice how well the white tip shows up at night with a torch beam played upon it. An alternative is to fix an isotope to the end ring but I find these play tricks with my eyesight after a while

In the winter, the sight of small fish dimpling the surface can often be the guide to bigger fish, predators especially, beneath them

If a bream has to be retained for a short while, to assemble a camera for example, it is a good idea to lay it in submerged weeds in this way

This bream fell at dawn. It was a perfect morning—dull, warm with a hint of drizzle and no wind

This was the smallest of the bream we took by far and a scale reading suggested it was a far younger fish as well. It is good to think the shoal could be breeding—though the fish could just be an escapee from a flooded river valley pit

When prebaiting, it is essential to put mashed bread in swims over 4 feet deep or with swans about, or the chub won't get a look in. Generally three or four slices of mashed bread is the right amount of bait to put into a fairly slow swim. This can be increased if you know there are a lot of fish about, or if the current is strong enough to carry the more buoyant pieces of crust away with it

Search for chub

Also in the great roaching days there were surprises other than the occasional bream. A big perch might fall to a maggot or worm, and every now and again a chub would come along. The lower Wensum was stocked with chub in the 1950s and 60s and these odd fish were the large pioneers, looking to spread ever further upriver. Certainly when they came along they were big: 5lb 2oz from the bridge by the County School; 4lb 14oz from the bend above Elmham Mill; 5lb 6oz from the rapids behind Worthing Pit. But never could I get my six-pounder, and though I hooked a handful around that mark something always conspired to let the fish break free. In June of 1989 I had reason to believe that this situation would be rectified at long last: Miller and I were prospecting some of the old haunts and though we saw no roach, here and there we did disturb a chub or two. On the point of an island we flushed out something enormous, and this, I was convinced, was the chub I was after; we baited it up steadily through June ready for the open season. After a good deal of bread had gone into the area around the island, I felt confident of giving the swim a try.

Roger baits up an excellent looking swim (above) where an overhanging tree makes a large slack. During the day, fish hide in the shelter of the branches. They will come out to feed as dusk falls, so it pays to get into the swim slightly before sunset (below). Fish may already be on the move and the setting sun can throw long shadows

This swim provides all sorts of features. There is a deep channel between the island and the bank. The current is steady rather than strong and there are a large number of overhanging trees

Even at the dead of night, you have to be constantly alert. The bite from even a big fish need only nudge the quivertip so slightly you first think it is a breath of wind. I keep my hand constantly around the reel handle, ready for an instant strike

The evening was a beautiful one—very clear and still after a parchingly hot day. The corn was already ripening and there were poppies on the lanes and around the hedgerows, all glowing in the sunset; there was to be a good moon and the night would never be truly dark. My hopes were high. I put mashed bread above the island, alongside it, and a hundred yards beneath it. Altogether six swims were baited and I planned on visiting each, every two hours, as the night progressed. Dusk. Owls. Darkness. Nothing. A fox walked past me and I started. I moved. Nothing. Midnight, and I suspected that I had a knock and I stared intently. Nothing. I moved again. And 2am. 4am, and the sky to the east began to glow. There was a sudden chill and I was glad of the quilted one-piece suit.

Now a mist develops over the cooling river and some swans begin to move my way. There is some surface activity and I tense up, standing by the rod. Nothing. 6am, and I move for the last time to the swim beneath the trees where the waterlilies crowd round the slack. Already it is another glorious day, and as the heat floods in I am back to my open shirt. Not a soul have I seen all night long, and now I am tired, sand-eyed, barely able to watch the quiver tip against the bright water. It's breakfast time and I know I am hungry, but perversely I stop on, probably too tired to move. I'm dreaming, surely, that my rod tip is moving round. But no! It *is* a fish, struggling hard to get to the lily roots. It's a chub I know by the feel of the fight, and when it rolls I know that this is a big one. I pile on pressure and up he comes, his great head shaking, sunlight bouncing off his scales. He's in the weigh sling. I breathe deeply and look hard. He's not six pounds by two meagre ounces. We look at each other, the chub and I, and I know it doesn't really matter that two, tiny, man-devised measurements have cheated me of my ambition. Anyway, I know that Nature can't be measured by fixed limits; she is too grand and too noble for that. So I bid the chub good morning and wish him a fond farewell.

Sunrise is an excellent time for chub, but try to face the sun so there are no problems with falling shadows. Also use as much reed cover as possible

The rising sun so often makes the river smoke like this—a condition that for some reason stimulates both chub and roach, especially in the summer

The white quivertip is most suitable for visibility in all conditions, and a position low to the water like this will register even the shyest of bites

When I made the swim, I was careful to leave a big growth of nettles between me and the fish downriver to my left. I am legering just on the point of the island 15 yards away, so should be invisible

The chub—just under the 6lb mark

Opposite: All river fish love lilies both for the shade they offer and also for the food that gathers around their stems and roots

This roach is a significant fish—apart from weighing almost 3lb 4oz. It was found by Roger Miller and me in a pit yards from the river. Obviously huge fish are still around and the Wensum can still deliver a surprise. Bill Giles, togged for pike, wonders if it could be used for bait! Bill is the dearest angling companion, and we all look forward to his company. He is also the only man I know who will use a deadbait all day long and go home, cook it and eat it—even if it has pike marks on it!

A hope for the future

I have just been fishing the river hard in this summer of 1990, and what I have seen has gladdened my heart. There are long stretches where the work of the dredger will probably never be undone, but in many places the abominable machine has been off for some years and maybe now, because of finance and environmental pressure, will stay off for good. In these areas the Wensum is slowly mending herself. Cattle are recreating their drinks, the true bed is showing through the algae, and wherever this happens, ribbonweed and roach begin to appear. In places there are many roach between ¼lb to 1¼lb, with some sightings of the few old 2lb chaps that gave them life. More than this, even, last year's fry still exist in abundance—now prime little fish of 2oz or so. A run of hot summers and mild winters has given them the high water temperatures and water stability that they have needed. Fallen trees have not been cleared, but have remained to give them shelter, and so little by little the story of doom is reversing itself. For my beloved river, after all these grey years, I now at last begin to see fresh hope for the 21st century.

Hope for the future: a young, fresh roach, spawned a year ago

PART III

The Summer Stillwaters

There is so much to an angler's life around the stillwaters of the summer, watching the waterside and the country at work. I have always loved the old gamekeepers, men like Tom up at Felbrigg; I admired his happiness in old age, his dog, and a quite small male tench that he landed on my rod. We often talked about his life as a keeper, in the evening as tench began to bite up at the surface of that lovely secluded lake of his. He was of a generation when everything on the estate would be killed, and only late in life was he beginning to realise there were other ways forward. A summer angler comes to know the farmers around him, the labourers and the water bailiffs—even the sheep shearers causing havoc with their dogs and the frightened flocks. Success in the summer often depends on spring fish-spotting, a time when the birds are nesting around the water fringes and in the woodlands.

During the long summer days that follow, intimacy with the lake builds; a friendship with a hedgehog that comes each night to be fed, shortly after the barn owl begins to quarter the fields at dusk. An angler comes to recognise each particular heron on his special beat, and the route followed by the grebe diving to feed its chicks. He is privileged to see fish that few other people even guess at: there is a buttercup yellow crucian carp, all hunky, chunky and adorable. There is a mysterious eel that breeds somewhere in the Atlantic. There is the rudd, so beautifully golden and scarlet that no artist could create him. There are the exotic fish like the golden tench and the koi carp—but nothing is more likely to remain in the memory than the summer carp. The carp is a hallmark of the summer: carp mouthing for crust or nosing towards floating baits; carp basking under trees; carp motionless in milk-warm water; carp bubbling in the shallows; carp rolling at the end of a line; carp ready for the net; carp well and truly beaten and held for a minute in startling clear light; carp then trekking over the scum of a hot evening lake; carp burrowing frantically for baits on the gravel bar. Carp fever is hardly surprising: they are beloved for their size, beauty and their visible cunning, and for many, many anglers they are the highlight of the summer.

Nature's beauties must not, however, blind anglers to her frailties. All smallwaters are fragile resources, and pits can be back-filled with rubbish, ponds can be drained for houses or roads, lakes may become silted and dried up, and the whole population of fish lost each time such a disaster happens.

Male and female tench are easily differentiated. The males have the pronounced bones protruding above the ventral fins which themselves are very large and deeply cupped. Males are also very much smaller than females the same age, often only half the size

This is an old shot taken when neither John Nunn nor I realised the harm knotted keepnets—indeed all keepnets—can do to fish. Numbers of fish should not really be kept at all, and individuals are best held in a carp sack

Tom's line of stoats at Felbrigg Lake many years ago. He used to compare this macabre sight to a fisherman's keepnet: 'You want to show off what you caught, boy.'

The summer stillwaters

A grebe on the nest

Hedgehogs are often attracted to anglers by the pieces of bait that are spilled. At night, they make a great deal more noise than their size suggests and their gruff, heavy breathing can be quite sinister

The barn owl in flight

The mark of the heron, the dawn fisherman who wastes as much as he takes

The crucian carp is easily differentiated from his bigger common carp cousins by his chubby shape and by the complete absence of barbules from the mouth. He is probably the shyest fish that swims: baits must be small, tackle delicate and presentation made before he bites

The behaviour of a diving grebe can be a very useful guide to the whereabouts of the smaller fish it feeds upon. Where you see a grebe diving repeatedly a shoal of roachlings or tiny bream are bound to be resident—along with the predatorial perch and pike

For me and many other anglers, the crucian carp is just about the prettiest fish that swims, and possibly the hardest to catch. They have very delicate feeding habits which makes them difficult, but then remember that they are members of the carp family: they are long lived with long memories

Rudd and roach very easily hybridise and a true rudd should have a protruding bottom lip, a golden sheen to its scales, a dorsal fin well down the back and a sharp edge to the body beneath the anal fin

Golden tench were introduced from Germany
in the nineteenth century and their numbers
have dwindled greatly over the years

A koi carp approaches a piece of floating crust
and, as usual, backs off again. When a koi
gets into the wild it almost invariably becomes
even more wary than its common or mirror
carp cousins. To catch one is indeed an
achievement

An absolute tragedy. This WAS one of the south's best rudd waters. The village nearby was extended, a bore hole was dropped and a lake that had taken scores of years to mature was a puddle by the end of the summer

This tiny pool is proof big fish can come from unlikely places. The vast amount of weed is a sign of prolific life and fish can be extracted if strong enough gear is used. Runs must be stopped quickly, or too much weed will collect on the line and the hook can easily pull out

Smallwater carp

No pool is too tiny for a big fish. Even today in a hectic, overcrowded world there are some still lost in secret ponds that are so small that they are neglected. One of only a third of an acre comes to my mind. It is covered almost constantly with weed and is neglected by everyone else who passes it. However, on a tip, I watched it hard through a summer day and found the water to be clear and healthy under the thick coating of pondweed. Into the gaps I put sweetcorn and sat back to wait. A kingfisher alighted on a branch near me and I was lost in the wonders of the wood.

Then there was a shape by the dam. Two or three fish. No, now a shoal of five or six fish. All feeding ravenously on the corn I had put in.

For neglected carp like these the most simple rig will suffice; an old quill and a few grains of corn threaded straight onto the hook are quite adequate. For me, there has not been carping like it for ages and that, if anything, is the beauty of it. I creep into position, and despite the heat I keep my shirt on for the camouflage it will give. The carp are throwing up bubbles until the water is in a froth. After only ten minutes my float trembles, lifts, trundles along the surface and is gone. The fight is all about keeping the fish from that pondweed and so all the action is on the surface. The pool rocks from side to side with the thrashing of the carp's tail. It is not an enormous fish by some standards, but is well into the teens of pounds and hugely satisfying from a pond no-one else had even dreamed of fishing.

Carp take large floating baits very carefully. They frequently mouth them repeatedly, feeling for line or a hook. Only the most cleverly presented piece of crust is taken, and even then it is probably broken up by the carp's fins as an extra precaution

A mass of smaller baits like these floating dog biscuits are treated quite differently. A lot of baits attract a group of carp, and there is immediately competition for the food. The carp have less time to inspect individual baits and there is more chance of a hook bait being accepted

On hot, still days, carp often laze in the surface film. They are rarely feeding but they can be tempted by well presented floating bait

Carp are great explorers of their environment. They love to search the margins, often feeding outside the water altogether!

Sweetcorn fed steadily into a clear hole gradually attracted the carp to feed. Their confidence built up slowly and I did not fish until they began to dig furiously for the grains. Then I felt I could almost guarantee a bite

In such situations, tackle need not be sophisticated. An old quill float and a hook with three grains of corn threaded straight on is quite adequate for fish feeding hard and close in. There is never any point in making rigs more complicated than they need to be

Whilst the tackle can be straightforward, the approach must be as careful as possible. One false move at this stage can spell the end of two hours' preparation

Little fights better than the hooked carp. Have confidence in your gear and be his master. If he gets into the weeds he will very probably be lost

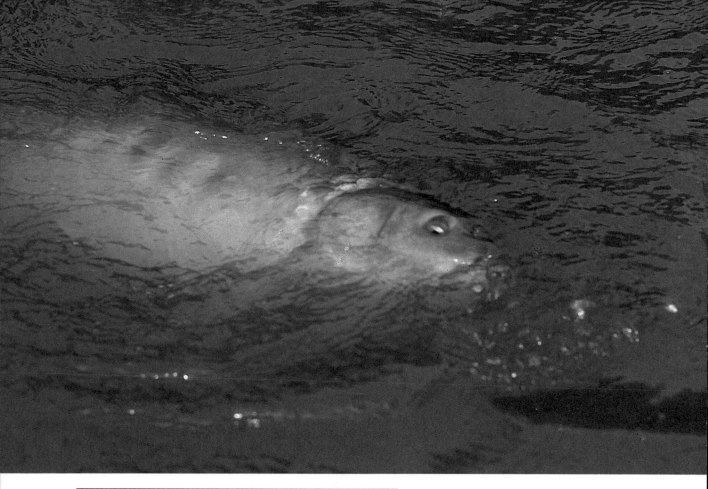

The carp fights long and hard, but once its head breaks surface a couple of times the fish should be beaten soon. The theory is that it takes in air that makes it more difficult for it to dive

The carp, ready for the net

Overleaf: A large carp from a small pool

Around the evenings of warm days, it is common to see lazing carp stir and move purposefully around the lake. It is now quite likely that some fish will go down on baits

Close observation is needed to see carp in a small, weedy lake

The kingfisher

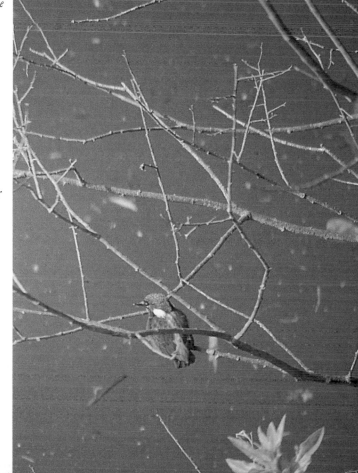

Only a carp can make a chap this happy!

A surprise 'grassie'!

More peculiar still were two hours spent on a beautiful lake situated this time in the heart of an old estate. Permission to fish there was only granted grudgingly, and I knew that I might only have one chance. Fortunately the first fish that I saw broke surface within two or three minutes. I looked at it very hard. Very hard indeed. Many years ago in a similar, protected water I saw some massive chub and wrote about them. A month later it transpired that these chub were in actual fact grass carp—a taste of exotica I obviously had never experienced. But that hardly helped my reputation as a fish sleuth! Still conscious of this old disgrace, I sat tight and watched the lake further. The day was very warm and shapes passed indistinctly here and there in the water in front of me, but without any definite further clues being given. Then I noticed a thistle flower on the surface, ten yards out. It travelled a short way and disappeared in a swirl. I broke off a piece of rush blade and this, too, drifted away from the bank. A shape. A mouth. A swirl—and then it was gone!

In high summer heat waves small waters can be difficult to fish. The shaded area under overhanging trees are often the most productive areas

A piece of reed is certainly the strangest bait I've ever used. A thistle head is plucked as an alternative!

On a whim I decided to try the lake with trout tackle, only substituting three inches of reed for a fly. Casting was not easy, but finally I forced my 'bait' five rod lengths out and then I waited. The wait was not for long and within five minutes or perhaps ten, my very first grass carp was struggling as I held it. Even the lively five minute fight into every corner of the lake hadn't subdued it.

Like the crucian carp, like the golden tench, like the koi carp, like the golden orfe and the big wild goldfish of some lakes, this gorgeous fish was a most welcome addition to the summer basket. All these fringe species, like grayling and dace from the rivers, like char from the lochs, give that bit of variety and interest to the whole angling scene.

Whenever possible keep low when playing a big fish close to the bank. He is already afraid of the tackle and the sight of the angler will only alarm him into redoubled escape efforts

The grass carp approaching the piece of reed . . . and caught!

A carp from the Boathouse Lake

Life in the summer of 1989 began in earnest on the Boathouse Lake—an estate of water of some five acres, gin clear, secluded, and holding a group of big, old, worldy-wise mirror carp. I knew that just to fish such water was a privilege, as I parked for a thirty-six hour session, and any fish taken would be a bonus.

As is my way, I left the gear behind in the car and spent the first hours wandering the banks with samples of baits. I moved with absolute care, for these are fish sometimes fearful and always very aware of man. As soon as an angler appears and makes his presence known, then the lake tenses up. Fish drop from view, fish hide in snags, fish sulk in the deeper holes. All normal carp behaviour ceases.

It was my first visit of the year after the good seasons I had enjoyed in '87 and '88 and I was alarmed by what met me. The hot summer after the dry winter had lowered the lake by twelve or eighteen inches, in few places were there more than three or four feet of water, and the colour of it had gone from crystal to diamond clear. Under a rising, hot sun, it was as though the water was not there at all, as though the patches of weed were grass waving in the wind and the big fish themselves hovering only in space.

The day was going to be hot, and I could tell that everything was going to be a struggle. I have always liked to get these fish in close and catch them on particles, and all through the day I pursued the carp round the margins watching their behaviour. Somehow, quite unnaturally, they were always aware of my presence. They would move nervously, without any of their usual confidence. If they did cross bait then they either sped away or at very best picked up a grain or two. Most times, they simply avoided baited areas altogether.

Later on in the afternoon I found the fish basking in the shallows, and once again they treated my nuts and maize with either disdain or apprehension. Floating baits were equally scorned, as usual. Dusk came and passed. Nightfall set in and there followed six hours of quiet darkness. A single fish swimming into my line broke my sleep.

I woke to find the exact same dawn of twenty-four hours before. If I were to fish the same way then I had no doubt that my results would be equally dismal. As the sun rose and the heat developed I was quite sure that once again the fish would hang far out in the shade of the island, a cast of some seventy to ninety yards. I had to abandon particles and move to a big bait now, but I shied from using the modern boilies for two reasons: on a natural water the boilies seemed superfluous; and secondly, practically, they take time to be recognised as food. I had neither the necessary time, nor the number of baits, nor the will to adapt the modern boilie approach. The oft-forgotten lobworm seemed to be my answer. Lobworms are visible and immediately attractive; in rain they flood into a lake like this. The carp here must have had millions in their long lives and I had confidence in the biggest, liveliest lob that I could fish now.

Deep in the forest, lobs were not hard to find even in the daylight and soon I had one, air injected to make it float, eighty yards away the far side of the island. It was 8am now, and I sat back to await events that glorious summer day.

Very good summer carping conditions. The sun is well masked by cloud but the absence of wind prevents the water being chilled. If the day is heavy and sultry with the promise of thunder, prospects can be excellent

At these times, the carp tend to swim very high in the water where they are likely to take floating baits

92

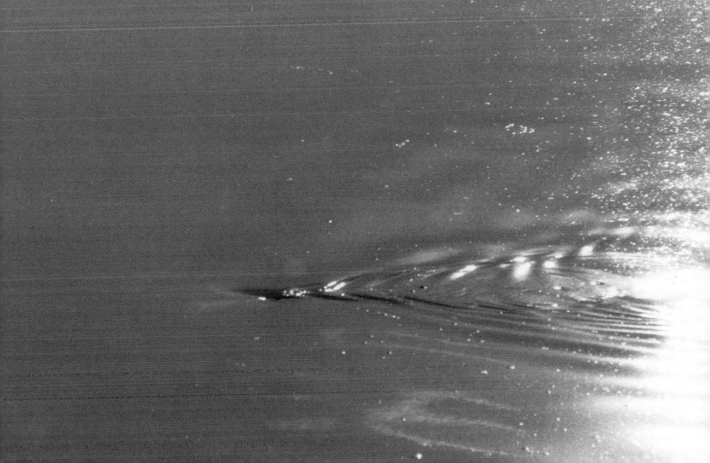

What an amazing sight for an angler—the golden tench breaks the surface and lights up the English countryside

Ugly to some, eels are beautiful to others. Certainly their life cycle is romantic. They are spawned in the far Atlantic and run into our rivers as needle-sized elvers. They make their way to a secluded pool where they might live for fifty or more years before returning thousands of miles to their birthplace to spawn and die

A structure like this on a lake can be invaluable for fish watching. Failing this, the serious angler will be forced back into climbing trees!

Very clear water and very bright weather make a carp angler's task very difficult

A carp came into picture on my left, high in the water, a lovely fish in the mid-20lb region I guessed. It approached my line that stretched tight to the island. Three yards away from it the fish slowed down; two yards away and it boiled, and at a yard, it surged over the line in fright and made off down the lake. I was badly shaken by this. I could not tempt fish in close, and at range they were afraid even of the line itself. It seemed that I was stumped this particular session.

Thank goodness the water was so low. Leaving my rod on the bank and the bail arm of the reel open, I carried the worm and the lead over to the island itself, wading always about waist deep, very slowly, in silt and warm water. At the island, I laid the worm five yards the far side, then tucked the line in close to the over-grown banking for twenty yards and finally trod the line from island to rod into the bottom weed as best I could. Now I hoped that hardly any line would be visible to passing fish. I dried off in the sun and sat back. At least I had a durable bait in a prime area with the line hidden for most of its length. Of course I worried that I had scared the carp for the day, or that the line might become entangled during any run-and-strike sequence that might follow.

I sat for hours, watching the far bank through my binoculars. Till noon the lake was dead, and not until 1pm did a back break surface. It was 3pm before the lake was anything like normal again—seven hours after my waded cast. Obviously by now the worm would be dead, and perhaps the air would have escaped. Would a fish accept the limp, long-dead worm, stretched out unappetisingly on the silt?

Typically the clear water close in is barren of fish and as is usual in carp fishing, a long cast to the trees of the far bank is almost essential. On the right is a large island and the mouth of the channel; between it and the far bank is a perfect ambush point. Binoculars are essential to pick out feeding fish at this range. If one is spotted, put a bait close to it at once

On the strike, really power the fish away from the far bank and all the fallen branches that offer sanctuary

The fish is making for the rear of the island and it must be stopped at all costs. Once steered into open water there should be few problems, providing the hook holds

A carp should be held steady until it is strong enough to swim away

Opposite above: A typical, agitated carp. It swims high and fast in the water, sensing that something is wrong

Opposite centre: The carp sees an angler's line and its agitation explodes as it prepares for evasive action

Opposite below: A carp frightened like this can take hours or even days to settle down and feed again. Worse still, it can alarm other fish in the water and put them on a kind of 'red alert'

Relief!

By 4pm several fish were moving around the island, and at 4.15pm I had my answer. I was training my binoculars on a fish that I guessed was very close to my bait. It showed little or no sign of tipping up, but the line suddenly tightened and the fish bolted. I ran back up the bank, striking as hard as I could, and the water erupted under the tree fringe ninety yards off.

I don't know what it is about the Boathouse Lake carp, but they fight harder than any I have ever known. Probably it is the clear shallow water and their own lean shape allied to proportionally massive fins. Whatever, I was shakingly grateful to find my fish at long, arm-achingly last, in the net.

The carp was a magnificent example of that very rare beast, the two tone. The tail half—let's say 13lb—was a deep brown, and the head half—another 13lb—was the lightest of sand colours. All I could think was that the fish had sunbathed the hot month past, standing on its head!

Big tench campaign

Roger Miller is an angler after my own heart. He will go days, weeks even, without fishing until the right challenge comes his way. And then he is unshakeable, after his prey till it should fall or he should equally obviously have failed. Only then will he rest again until the next angling adventure comes to his mind. Of all fish, probably tench are his favourite and the possibility of a Norfolk seven-pounder excited him, as it rightly should. If we forget these 'nines' and 'doubles'—the monsters of the Home County gravel pits—and get tench back into their real historical perspective, we will realise that a four-pounder is a good fish, a five-pounder is excellent, a six is a fish of a lifetime and a seven is a dream. Above that and the angler must go to Kent!

Roger chose to fish now for a Norfolk 'seven' simply because he saw one. In the crystal clear lake, three-, four-, and five-pounders abounded, but one very large fish indeed kept on their fringe, following them over a two hundred yard length of bank always keeping slightly aloof. This fish Roger and I judged to be some seven pounds—perhaps even a little more. Roger's most serious attempt coincided with a high summer Tuesday morning.

Roger was already there when I arrived a little after first light. The weather was obviously going to be unreliable. There had been heavy overnight rain and though the sky was now clear, storm clouds lay off a little down wind. Indeed within minutes, rain belted down and we were forced to shelter under the boughs of a well leaved tree. As we waited for the next band of blue, Roger explained his plan to me. He would bait reasonably heavily ten yards out with cereal, corn and hemp to stop the main body of the tench. Closer in at five or six yards he would bait very sparingly and tightly to interest the big girl who travelled alone. In this latter patch he would obviously lay his own float-fished bait.

The rain cleared and Roger got back to the lakeside. Things, for once, went to plan. By 7am he had a dozen good-sized fish feeding over his further pitch, and at 8am the big girl appeared, milling around, nervously on the edge of the action. Twice she approached Roger's close-in pitch, and once it seemed that she stopped to investigate. Then, more clouds appeared, the light values sank and we were left, literally, in the dark. It began to drizzle around the float that shortly before had been hallowed in sunbeam. Perhaps we noticed a bubble coming up nearby and once possibly the float lifted a little, suspiciously; but my eyes were set firmly on the horizon where blue again showed beyond the grey. It was then, quite suddenly, that Roger struck. For a second we doubted if it was the big fish, but then she picked up pace and made off to the middle of the lake, the way all the big ladies tend to do. And, of course, there was no stopping her on a three-pound hook length and a size 16 hook that carried the single grain of corn: Roger simply had to go with her, give her line and let her tire herself at range. For a good while the fight went as Roger planned. The tench was plainly the big one by the way she moved, majestically and unstoppably, but she did nothing untoward and yard by yard, Roger retrieved line. Twenty yards out, however, disaster threatened to strike. The tench moved slowly left, and any pressure that Roger applied pulled her off course *in towards* the massive reed bed. It was not that she was actively seeking it as sanctuary, simply her run and the rod's power combined to dictate such a course. Roger slackened the pressure off. She continued left, however, closing all the time towards those reeds and her escape.

Roger Miller holds a Norfolk 'seven'

It is a good idea to fish facing sunrises—and sunsets—to avoid a shadow being cast. Also, keep down low beneath the line of rushes along the bank

During the showers, the water was too dark for us to see what the fish were doing

In clear water, tench are plain to see. They tend to move in small groups and will settle on bait for a few minutes before continuing with their patrols of the bank. Tench do not always send up bubbles or stir up silt. Both these tench are feeding hard with no change in water clarity

Very large tench like this often travel and feed alone. Here, she has just picked up two or three grains of corn that can be seen around her

There is simply no better way of fishing for tench up to about 20 yards out than floatfishing. Windbeater floats and Drennan crystal floats are both excellent and should be shotted down to about ½ inch from the surface. The bite is likely to be a very sharp dip so it pays to have a hand on the rod all the time

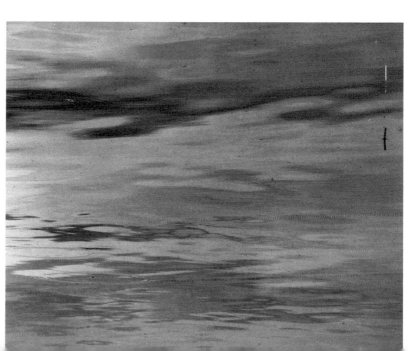

You will notice here that I am holding the handle close to the net and that my hand is around the net's spreader block to lend extra support. A big tench and wet mesh is quite a load on a slender frame

There was only one answer. The fish was nearly beaten and I would have to go in, in front of the reeds, and net her there as she wallowed. Still yards from the outer reed fringe and the water lapped at the top of my waders; a further step and seepages over the top increased, but it came almost as a relief once I *was* wet and could plough on regardless. I could see the line three yards out from me, then the float two yards from the reeds and then the giantess herself swirling on the lip of safety. I hurried forward, then steadied myself, dipped the net, prayed and lifted. That was where you wanted to see all good tench and the float that caught them, in the bottom of the net! I waded back in triumph. Roger relieved me of the fish and hurried away from the water for the weighing.

And were we right? Did that tench make the cherished seven pounds? Not by a whisper, I am afraid. But she was magnificent. On cue the sun burst through again and she went back gleaming dark gold. I don't think Roger fished again for a month!

Roger Miller releasing his near 7lb tench

106

A big tench like this can often be twenty to thirty years old and has seen every angling trick in the book. Your approach has to be just a little bit special to keep ahead of her ever extending experience

The micromesh landing net does not harm the tench's scales or fins

During mornings of cloud and rain, tench can feed on until well after midday, especially when there is a good ripple. On this particular day, there is a perfect warm wind from the south

A summer's day on the lake

Generally, a tench or bream angler concentrates on the short, intensive period at the waterside, perhaps at dusk or dawn. However, every now and again it is good to spend from dawn to dusk—say, 4am till 10pm—at the lake. A good deal can happen in eight hours . . .

Dawn often comes in cold, especially near the coast where a wind blows in fresh from the sea. And that was how it was when I found Martyn, dressed securely against the elements, preparing to use his open end feeders for the tench and perhaps even the bream.

A bream bag

There is no better feeder fisherman than Martyn: he takes great care with the ground bait that plugs the open ends, mixing it to just the right texture with various aromatic additives. He works two rods, casting very frequently in the same area always, building up the swim with feed and attracting the fish. Everything is handily laid out, and after years of experience, is just where whichever hand wants it. His pitch really is a mix of tidiness and chaos—especially now, when a bream shoal has moved in.

Martyn Page shows exactly how to set up for a swimfeeder session. The optonics and rod rests are in firmly and close to the water. The landing net is in readiness. The sweetcorn is out of its can in a big container for ease of access. The groundbait to plug the ends of the feeder is made up next to the corn and is of the exact consistency, colour and aroma. Plastic overtrousers are a good idea to keep the slime and bait away from clothing

The dawn approaches

This is how to weigh a bream—in a wet, nylon sack

Opposite above: Martyn begins a session by casting a rod out repeatedly so that the feeder lays down a good carpet of bait. Soon the bream appear, drawn by the splashes and by the smell of the bait. Soon, too, they will go down and begin to feed

Opposite below: Martyn strikes. He avoids twitches and small lifts on the bobbin. These are probably line bites, caused by the big flat body of the bream catching the line and giving a false indication. Striking at these only disturbs the entire shoal. It is better to wait until the bobbin hits the butt and the reel actually begins to revolve. This takes patience and nerve but the fish will be on!

The wind has probably stirred them, and thirty yards out from Martyn's platform the clear water begins to muddy as bream go down over the ground bait. The shapes of fish can be seen browsing and then disappearing into the clouded water. Bites come thick and fast, often within seconds of casting out the feeder. By mid-morning Martyn is working like a dervish to keep the two rods going and to put in enough feed to hold the bream in front of him. And, of course, each bream has to be played, landed, weighed sometimes and returned. (It is inhuman to keep big bream in a keep net for any length of time. Certainly that particular morning proved that returning them to the water does not mean the end of sport.) The whole platform began to look like a battleground, and the two little Mitchell reels were caked in the ground bait and sweetcorn juice. I almost felt it was something of a relief when late morning came, the wind died and the skies cleared, and a blistering hot day emerged, causing the bream to rise up in the water, look restless and begin to drift away. Only thirty minutes after the sun broke through, the water was going clear again, and the bream could be seen moving away south towards the shallows.

A good specimen

Martyn was constantly at work casting, striking, reeling in feeders and fish. He hardly ever sits down whilst the shoal is with him and by using a long hook length, bream often took the bait on the drop through the water

A passing swan

Stalking

That is where John Nunn and Roger Miller were fishing. Their approach was somewhat different—almost a coarse fishing version of flyfishing! In the clear water they were watching small groups of bream criss-crossing the shallows, casting lobworms two or three yards in front of them so they slowly sank as the fish passed. Roger was using a bubble float half filled with water to give casting weight, though a carp surface-fishing controller float would have done equally as well. John was using a small ledger weight to get the bait out, and was watching the line in the water for bites: when the line lifted or slackened, he struck and often to good effect. This was a most exciting form of fishing and called for great concentration, intense observation and casting accuracy. Both men were picking up bream regularly, and John especially landed a lovely male bream with the white spawning tubercles still on its head. The bailiff came down to admire it, his pipe puffing contentedly up into the blue skies that surrounded the fine park trees.

My own morning fared less well. Roger joined me, put out some bait and immediately attracted the swans. I left him to them and headed away to the furthest shallows where I hoped to track down a possible large carp.

Below left: This style of fishing calls for intense concentration and certainly polaroid glasses. It is a good idea too to hold the line and feel for bites that sometimes cannot be seen

Below right: John wades out to get a better view of the fish. Providing you stay still on your feet, fish will come in quite close

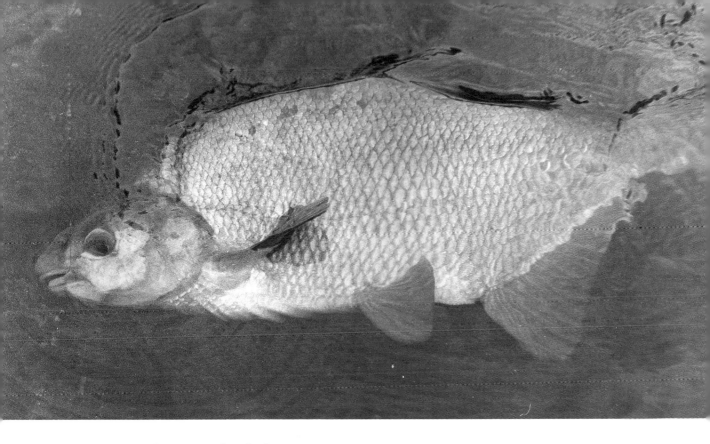

A bream comes to the net . . . and reaches it

John admires the bream

Immediately more problems arose. The swim I wanted appeared to harbour a Spanish galleon! Novel! I continued down the lake and by early afternoon things were looking promising again. I hid in the reeds and began to stalk a good-sized common carp. I was certainly hidden from the fish, and from all the world as well, it seems—twenty yards away from me a young lady came to the water's edge, removed just about all her clothing and swam off over the shallow water. Of course, that signalled the end of my carp activities . . . a problem or not, that is the question?!

The sun now was very high and hot. John Nunn had left; Martyn and Roger were snoozing somewhere under the trees, and I decided to do the same until the shadows should lengthen over the water and the tench begin to move once more at evening time.

When I awoke, Martyn was already fishing. It was a superb evening and tench were already bubbling in his swim—before I even tackled up, Martyn was playing his first of the new session. As he held it a second, it mirrored the sunset, making a perfect image of the summer. I only wished that a picture could have conveyed also the song of the pigeon, the first warbling call of the tawny owl and the blissful smell of the hay meadow half-harvested.

For myself, the one reward of the evening was a very pleasant bream, the only fish of my own I had in fact netted in eighteen hours. But with all that had gone on, that was quite enough for me. Then as the sun sank, finally we were all off to the low-beamed pub, our backs sun-sore under our shirts, for at least two pints over stories of the day.

*Waterfowl are problems for the angler.
We have a duty not to interfere with
them so the best idea is to find deeper
water where swans at least cannot
reach the bottom*

Don't ask me . . . !

Martyn playing the tench

This is the most desperate moment of a fight. A fish has turned from the open water and is heading into the reed fringe. If it gets there the line will be broken, so heavy pressure must be exerted at once. The longer the run develops the harder it will be to stop and turn

Martyn brings the fish into the net

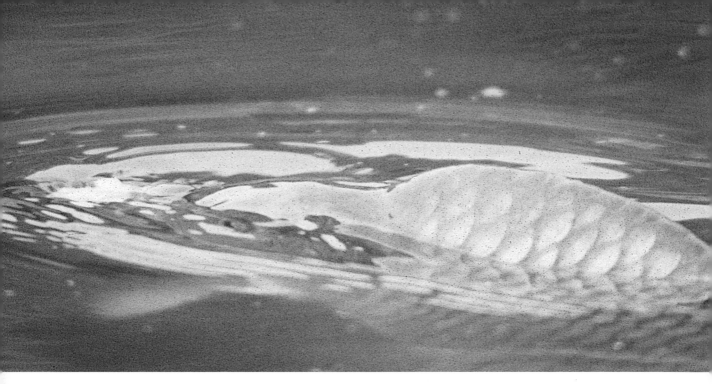

Above: Common carp in the water   *Below: Martyn's tench, caught in the evening session*

My one success of the day

*How every summer
evening should end . . .*

PART IV

Winter Predators

Piking in Broadland

A Broadland dawn, well into March, the last Sunday of the season in fact, and John Nunn and Steven Rouse meet at their boat on the reed-fringed River Thurne. The grey sky looks promising. The day is mild and the drizzle will come to nothing serious. Both men have lives of Broadland fishing behind them and they know this is the time of year when a really great female fish could fall. A big female in March, heavy in spawn, probably in a group of similar fish is what every piker dreams of finding. Fish like this have been located in the past and they have become history. Thirty pounders. Forty pounders. There are still those who believe a fifty pound fish could come from the Thurne or its Broads, Hickling, Horsey, Heigham or Martham North Broad.

The armoury of gear that the two men bring to the boat is impressive: a petrol engine to power the boat miles along the river on the Broadland system; an electric engine to trickle the boat along noiselessly when trolling; and a pair of oars to pole the gliding boat into shallow, reeded bays where the big, mottled girls could be lying. Then there are the rods, reels, tackle bags, bait and trappings of the normal piker's day.

There is just a touch of wan sunlight showing as they set out, enough to pour yellow into the sky and the waters beneath, enough to give the windmill's bricks a little warmth—and then even this faint ray dies. The drizzle returns. It is pushed on by the north wind, and you taste the slightest tang of salt in the moisture; the sea is only a couple of miles away and perhaps it is the slightly saline content of the system that breeds such large fish. Or the bream shoals. Or the vast lonely spaces that allow the pike to ghost here and there at will and to disappear for seasons on end from the pursuing anglers.

John and Steven troll down the river, very slowly, very quietly, pulling two small roach behind them. The river hardly flows, just rocking gently between the tightly reeded banks. There are no other boats on the water. The silence of the morning is complete.

They go past Martham South Broad, its opening firmly wired off and warnings against fishing everywhere in view. This is a nature reserve and vital for the shelter of bird and plant life. The Broad is also the impregnable sanctuary of those big pike that have been frightened off the rest of the system by angling pressure. There is not a pike angler alive who would not die for a day on the South Broad— they all know twenty and thirty pound pike abound there. This is the ultimate pike water in the country, and yet here the fish lie secure, protected from all but the few most unscrupulous of anglers. Poaching the Broad is not a temptation

Notice how the electric outboard makes no disturbance at all behind the boat. This is essential in shallow waters where even oars can spook fish

Big pike will always seek out sanctuary in a water—any area that the angler cannot get a bait to. Here, the safety of the pike is almost guaranteed—and they know it

Bill Giles holds his own fish-of-a-lifetime 30-pounder that fell when he was well into his seventies and after over a half a lifetime of trying!

Floating weed and miles of reed beds demand that the Broadland waters are fished by boat

Bittern chicks—as well as pike—make the Thurne region a valuable environmental asset

Geese flight into a broad at dawn—a time that sees probably the hardest feeding session of the piker's day

genuine anglers ever feel, but there *are* those who would put success before anything else in life. Richard, the warden of the marshes, knows this, and keeps a
hawk-like eye on the water. Even at night he patrols, catching men who care nothing for wildlife and the concerns of the environment.

Today Richard is lower down the river, stacking the reeds he has already cut
into a boat to be taken to the thatcher. The sky turns a shade more gloomy and the
drizzle becomes a light rain; but still the pike do not feed. Harriers quarter the
marshes, herons pass over towards the sea, and on the windmill arms cormorants
look out for their meal.

John and Steven reach Candle Dyke and turn up towards Heigham. Still without fish, they motor along Meadow Dyke and into the windswept acres of Horsey
Mere. There are several boats hugging the reed fringe. Martyn Page, a well known
pike-man, is on his own at the top of the Broad, whilst halfway down Steve
Harper, the captor of several thirty pound pike in the past, sits the day out. At the
mouth of the Broad that most notorious of Broadland pikers and the captor of a
huge thirty-eight pound fish, John Watson, sits cocooned against the weather.
Everybody is here searching for a taste of immortality, a fish to rock angling history, but none has caught a thing they will tell us about. Nor have Steve and John,
trolling slowly over the flats as midday approaches.

*This is a perfect piker's day. The light levels are low and there is a good chop on the water. The wind
however is warm and there is nothing to stop pike feeding all day long*

Life on the broads

Looking up Heigham Sound, cloud can be seen along the North Sea coast. This could push inland, kill the sunlight and improve the chances. Unfortunately, it could be driven by a cold, northerly wind which would be a blow to sport

Back they go down Meadow Dyke, searching bays here and there, meticulously, precisely, with small float-fished deadbaits. Bay after bay yields nothing until finally, John's float disappears in a heavy swirl. The fish fights well, too well really, for the truly big girls keep deep and slow and react only with solid power. Still, she is a well-built fish around seventeen pounds in weight and, more vitally, could be the pointer to her bigger sisters. However, an hour passes in the bay with no further sign of fish, and the two men again begin to troll the main river.

The light is going quite quickly, the afternoon gathers speed towards dusk and Steven's bait is taken. This is obviously a better fish. She follows the boat steadily, thumping the rod tip occasionally, but for the most part keeping doggo and obstinately deep. Just once, right by the boat, she comes and swirls alongside, showing her long, leopard-spotted flanks. She is a big fish, but as she sounds again the line flutters limp: the hooks have pulled out of the great boned jaw.

A lot of big pike waters are notoriously slow and the angler can do little but get there at dawn and resign himself for a stay till dusk. The temptation is to move after a few biteless hours but that one massive fish in the area might just be coming onto feed. Steve has a couple of deadbaits out, knows he is in a good swim historically and is content to let fate takes its hand

John Watson anchors further from the reed beds so that he can cover water in a 360 degrees arc of his boat. This half light in early afternoon is ideal

The petrol outboard is useful if the electric engine runs out of battery and the mud weight in front of John is the standard anchor type on the Broads

John brings his 17-pounder to the boat, and hoists it aboard. Note that the net is lifted in by its arms. The great weight of pike and wet mesh would otherwise break the net off at the pole fitting

The big fish neared the boat

The gathering dusk

Steven's lost fish

A very clear sunset can be a problem. It will probably bring down temperatures quickly and perhaps bring on an early frost. If the angler is prepared to fish on late, well into dark, a fish or two could fall later on

135

More time is spent trolling the area of the take, but again, she appears to have been a lone fish and there is no more action. There is just one card left to play: up a boat dyke a group of small male pike—jacks—are known to exist. It is just possible that a big female may have moved in with them as her spawning time approaches. The boat creeps up the dyke soundless as a white swan. The gloom of a dark marsh night is pulling in fast when at last the float goes. Ten seconds of wild optimism flow until the jack pike is felt, kicking frenetically at the end of the line. He is released, and with him go just about the last hopes of the season. The day has been intensely interesting, and both men have known that at any moment on such a water a real crocodile of a fish could have fallen to their boat. All session long there has been a tingling excitement, an anticipation, a subdued feeling that a massive Thurne fish could be close. How big was Steven's lost pike? Eighteen pounds he thinks—playing down the loss. Very probably it was larger—five pounds or so larger. Failing a true Thurne monster she would have been a fulfilling end to the 1990 pike season. Thoughtfully, the boys pack the boat away and look out over the marshes lost now to the night.

Below left: The pike is lifted from the net

Large female pike like this do not struggle and cavort in the way of jacks. Laid on their backs, their mouths open easily for the hooks to be removed. Held firmly under the gill flap and by the vent, they pose placidly for a photograph

A day with perch

When pike mania strikes Norfolk from October onwards, everything else gets neglected. Life revolves around collecting baits, preparing traces, maintaining boats and engines and setting alarm clocks for inhuman hours. Perch fishing is by contrast very much more relaxed. The appeal of perch is considerable. They feed off and on throughout the day and not just at dawn and dusk. Tackle can be light, baits are small and success can sometimes be pretty well instantaneous. And they are beautiful fish. The perch disease of the 1960s and 1970s was a tragedy for angling. Water after water lost its perch stocks and there are today younger anglers who have never even seen the splendid, bristling fish. Not all waters have recovered, and even now the problem is finding perch water that you have belief in. Rumours abound, and often the only way to find out is to try for yourself. unless you are fortunate enough to see the perch striking at shoals of summer fry. The only other rule I have found to be constant is that where there are small perch then the chances of at least some big ones are high.

So, find Roger Miller and me at dawn on a new lake not having a clue what to expect. It is a typical winter's day in drab west Norfolk, and light comes grudgingly about 7am. By 7.05am our four floats are out, buoyant enough to take one or two swan shot with the bait, lip-hooked on a size 6 or 8 single and set to swim in mid-water or slightly below. There is no better way, in our experience, to tackle a new water. Small live baits are instantly attractive, and fished like this, they drift over large areas as the wind pushes the line.

Dawn becomes a grey morning and nothing happens. By 10am we are wondering if the information we have received is correct, and ponder a move across the county to a known perch pit and an afternoon of possible action. But we stay: faint heart never won anything worthwhile in fishing, and we talk about life—that is, fishing—in the lee of a screen of poplar trees.

There is not much anybody can do to hurry perch. Spinning might help, or it might scare a wily old fish in the clear water conditions. We cast here and there around the lake, varying the depths the baits swim at, and Roger tries particularly hard under the branches of the bramble bushes on one side of the pool. Deep down, though, we know that patience is all.

Around midday we feel more confident, as on many perch waters lunch for man and fish coincides. It is not so here. The afternoon creeps onward.

It is hard to know what happens underwater, what strange mysterious switch is clicked on that gives the angler instant excitement. We know that for long hours perch will lie unmoving in the roots of old lilies, or sheltered in the masonry of a toppled wall or boathouse. Then something—hunger, a change in light values, the vibration of a prey shoal, a rise in air pressure or something equally unguessed at— triggers them into action. Their dorsal fins rise aggressively, rather like the erect tail of a cat which twitches as it stalks along grasses; the fins begin to work, and the angle of the perch subtly alters. From lying horizontally, or even nose downwards, they rise from the bed a little, heads pointing upwards as though scanning the upper regions for prey. Now they are in the strike position, and anything above them risks being taken.

Quite suddenly, at around 3.30 pm, our lake becomes alive. A float scurries two yards to the right and plops under. It stays there five seconds and bobs up again. The bait is inspected. It has been killed, but not ripped and cut by pike teeth—

A glorious sunset

Even large pike can be landed like this by the confident angler. It avoids any possibility of the hooks flying free and tangling in the net mesh where they can cause injury to both fish and angler

Pike men will fight through anything

The perch is a purpose-built predator. Its bold stripes afford it camouflage in dead branches and its mouth opens wide enough to engulf prey one third of its own weight

A shoal of scattering fish like this is a giveaway for the predator hunter. A pike could be responsible but here two or three larger swirls are visible, indicating that shoaling perch is the attracting species. Sometimes the spined dorsal fin of larger perch can be seen cutting the water

A perfect perch dawn will be still, warm and windless with a fair amount of cloud

Two swan shot keep the bait down and give enough weight for casting. When a perch attacks, it does not puncture the bait like a pike, but rather scuffs the scales off and perhaps threads the fins

A perfect perch swim will probably contain dead weeds that harbour the fry on which they feed. The perch lie just out in deeper water making periodic forays in for food

Fallen tree branches are another ideal perch haunt. In fact, big perch will rarely, if ever, be found far away from underwater obstructions of some kind

rather it is scuffed in patches as though the scales have been scraped from it. A typical perch take. Another float goes, and in the clear water we watch a big perch fighting against the bewildering force from above. The bait hangs perilously from its lips, the tail showing as the perch always takes its prey head first. The second fish falls. Then four more come, all in half-an-hour before darkness pulls in. We pose very briefly with the fish and watch them back into the lake. Six fish for fourteen pounds all on a half tip, on a bit of a hunch. This, though, is the way with perch waters. The angler today has got to believe enough and want perch enough to risk discomfort and blanks in his quest.

The bait, scuffed and damaged by a pike   *Opposite: The perch has a beautiful, and unusual, dorsal fin*

The perch fighting in the water (opposite). This is a perilous moment (right). The bait is working out of the perch's mouth and could come astray at any moment. Pressure is maintained, but slackened ever so slightly, as the fish is guided to the net

The perch takes the bait under the surface

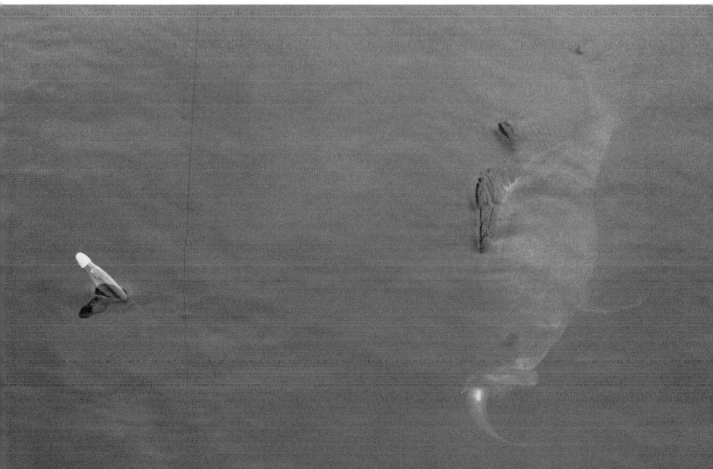

The beaten fish is steered to the net

Opposite above: A good pair of perch

Opposite below: The perch and the bait

Roger with our catch

Night trolling

There are times when pictures need hardly be amplified by words. Let me say, however, that the night session in focus took place in Wroxham, in the heart of Broadland tourist land—restaurants, bars, boatyards, riverside chalets—you name it, Wroxham has it in greedy abundance. It also has pike. Pike that are drawn here winter after winter in pursuit of the roach and bream shoals that shelter in the boatyards during the day and drop out to feed in the main river at night. The pike have been fished for many times over the years, and for most anglers they prove stubbornly difficult. Yet Chris Turnbull and his boat partner John Sadd have found a way to the heart of the matter. A boat and electric outboard are musts. Thereafter, they float-fish small live baits, set slightly over-depth, and trail them very, very slowly behind the quietly moving boat. And it's all done at night!

We launched by the road bridge under a rising full moon. It was a Saturday night and we passed the riverside inn alive with music, light and carefree weekend laughter. Downriver, where the river became darker between the empty holiday chalets, Chris put up the rods. The plan was to trail two baits some twenty or thirty yards behind the boat a couple of miles downriver and back again—docking at 10.30pm exactly. Important timing for three thirsty anglers!

The importance of the electric engine cannot be overstressed. It is virtually noiseless and creates none of the disturbance of a petrol motor or even a man on the oars. The boat felt as though it were pushed by the hand of some invisible water giant.

We had gone a quarter of a mile, and past a flock of swans ghostly in the moonlight, when the clutch of Chris's reel gave out line. The boat was stopped. The second rod was reeled in and Chris hit into something that immediately felt big. All was tension in the boat. All right, Chris could lift it from the bottom but only for the fish to sound again. He was looking worried, and we lit him a cigarette to calm the nerves. John worked the boat back towards the fish and under pressure it began to surface. By now tension had turned to puzzlement, and then an old eel trap, fairly hooked, surfaced and was hoisted aboard. John even fumbled for the scales . . .

On downriver we went, past a bungalow where two rods were fishing from a jetty with no angler in sight. Or was there. Across a lawn the windows shone with light and the back of a head could be seen watching a television. We gave one line a pull and the bite alarm sounded loudly. The head never moved. Television was all-consuming and we left the angler at peace. The story goes that another angler another night was so incensed with this same situation that he took one of the lines downriver a hundred yards and tied it firmly to a tree on the opposite bank. When the programme was over the armchair angler found himself hooked into a monster, something unstoppable, something that broke him off hopelessly in the darkness . . .

Again, it was Chris's rod that shrieked to a taking fish. Anxiously, Chris

It is hard to believe that such a busy place attracts pike but they come here after the roach shoals that are drawn into the security of the town's boatyards. At night, the roach enter the river to feed and there they meet the hungry pike.

All Chris's rods are ready made up and simply need joining together for instant action. A boat at night is not the place to set up pike tackle

Above: The eel trap comes aboard

Below: John with the scales

Chris watches his rod tip carefully. It shows up well against the slightly lighter sky and from its arc Chris can see which way the fish is running

watched the rod against the moon, and yes, it was throbbing and juddering to the kick of a fish. It circled the boat, illuminated by the torch beam, and then was unhooked carefully on the piles of soft rubber matting and wet nets. It was a fifteen pounder and the night was turning out well.

Away from the town, the river grew totally quiet and the only light source now was the moon. This was more like the night fishing I have known all my life, and a second slightly smaller pike fell. A watch face caught momentarily in the torch light and three worried anglers realised that a retreat upriver was thirstily called for.

The bar was crowded with fishermen, nearly all resident there since nightfall after fishless dawn 'til dusk days on the river. 'Any good, lads?' We smiled and listened to the gossip of the Broadland piker scene. Night pike. This now must be a real option for hard waters where the pike have seen every other trick.

151

The fish approaches the boat . . . and is landed

Miller's big pike

The Flyfisher's Pit in mid-Norfolk is a large, crystal clear lake run as a trout fishery and stocked regularly with browns and rainbows. This alone makes for big pike, but so does the club policy of removing all the pike caught—those that remain have the chance to grow enormous. Piking is only allowed for a week towards the Christmas period and for years, despite the desperately slow sport, it has been fishing that neither Roger Miller nor I would miss. And even considering the few great days in the past, 18 December 1989 was going to prove extra special.

We arrived at the water at 5.30am, two hours before first light. Seventy-odd-year-old Billy Giles was already there, and probably had been since early December, such is the dear old man's optimism. Jim Tyree and Brian Godfrey appeared at 6am, Dave Plummer and Ritchie Furlong at 6.30am, and Reg Sandys, the latecomer, at 9.30am.

Initially the wind was from the south-west, but during the morning turned round and became a north-easterly. There was good humour all around the lake. Dave Plummer fished with Ritchie under an umbrella the size of a house, with his breakfast cooking, the video camera at the ready, a portable phone should business call and bed chairs the size of four-posters!

There was some talk about the possibility of a real monster. Many were dubious, but after a relatively quiet three years or so I stuck to my belief that a big fish was due. That was why Miller and I were there. After all, we all knew what the water had produced in the past, and if the environment becomes more favourable then the pinnacle becomes that much greater.

Around 1pm Mrs Miller and Baby Miller came to visit; a few minutes later my own Joy arrived. After a while Mother and Baby left, however, Roger seeing them off hesitantly, for the swim had begun to show signs of life.

The facts thereafter are well known around Norfolk and make for a great deal of amusement. Simply, at 3.25pm my own dearly beloved decided to leave. Between our position on the lake and her car, however, lurked some of the county's notorious scoundrels: no man would trust a girl with Jim, Dave, Brian or Ritchie, and for her own honour and reputation I felt I had to escort her to the car park. We walked briskly to the club house, I extracted her from a one-piece suit and saw her safely off, and got back to the rods at 3.31pm.

There was Roger on his knees over the net, extracting *my* hooks from a giant! The video camera was rolling. The pike was hoisted to the scales and the rest is 39½lb of history. Soon after the jokes started: 'What shade of green were you?' 'Off you go to the pub, John boy, I'll look after the rods!' 'There's a sausage sandwich for you, John, if you're not too sick to eat it.'

It was all rather bizarre. After all, in those seven days I had spent sixty-six and a half hours on the water and been away from the rods for six and a half minutes. That I work out to being nearly a 700–1 chance against missing a run. Did I feel cheated by fickle fortune? Possibly on the morning after, when I woke at 5.30am and for just a moment was tempted never to visit the lake again; but the feeling subsided after a mile of the journey there. After all, I had seen a magnificent pike, a fish no words can do justice to. A photograph is all that is necessary; let Nature herself speak. There is another point: if Miller and Bailey say they are a partnership, then that is exactly what they mean—a partnership in good and bad. In angling partnerships glory is shared, pain is halved and jealousy is non-existent,

A dead still, bright dawn with a hard frost and a skim of ice can be the hardest of conditions. Deadbaits are often quite useless and a livebait only stands a chance of being taken

Rods set up, Kevin Grix can prepare a huge breakfast, and Dave Plummer prepares to ring into his tackle shop! Angling nineties' style! Even though they are otherwise engaged, the drop off bite alarms will alert them to the slightest movement at the bait end of things

My goddaughter asks to learn how to tie a trace!

Roger's massive pike

particularly as the purpose of the Flyfisher's Lake has always been to catch a very, very special fish. Dozens of dire, dull days have been our lot, but this once, *we* won through.

It is interesting now to ponder what did happen in that swim of ours between 1.30 and 3.30. In the first forty-five minutes Roger had four bits of action, when the baits went frantic, the floats dipped briefly—the first time for hours—and a couple of baits came back ripped, the obvious gashes of pike teeth. Nothing, though, absolutely nothing, developed into a strikable run—had we not known the swim, and had we not been fishing floats, we might well have been unaware of the whole episode.

From 2.15 to 2.30 there was a good deal of activity around the bank. Baby Miller began to totter around our pitch, myself following with a protective umbrella; this, and cold, feet-stamping ladies are not good things to have on the skyline of a gin-clear pit when you are fishing at a range of ten yards and by all rights, the roach-piercing culprit should have moved off. It did not, however. My own belief is that this one great pike came into the swim alone for two hours and lay there untroubled, hardly hungry, terrorising our baits that he treated with caution and disdain mixed. The period of disturbance above him on the bank passed, and only then did he strike with real purpose. Perhaps the light had died to the ideal limits. Perhaps the roach twisted provocatively and triggered the predatorial instinct. Perhaps the bait was presented in exactly the right manner, or place, or depth, or perhaps the big fish simply felt hunger, anger, or both. No other pike followed that large one that day, even though the baits went back in. I am pleased in a way that that was the case—any other fish would have been an anti-climax, and that one monster is likely to be the largest that any of us present on that fateful day will ever see in the rest of our lives.

This swim is a particularly good one. Very close in, a deep channel follows the bank and pike shoals wander along it when they are in feeding mood. Float paternostered livebaits set to swim in mid-water or just below stand a very good chance of stopping them and attracting a take

Acknowledgements

I would dearly like to thank Jim Tyree, Chris Shortis, Chris Turnbull, John Nunn, John Sadd and Roger Miller for all their photographic and angling help.

INDEX

Numbers in *italics* indicate photographs